Always My Son

Charlotte S. Snead

Always My Son
Hope House Girls Series
Charlotte S. Snead

Published May 2017
Little Creek Books
Imprint of Jan-Carol Publishing, Inc.
All rights reserved
Copyright © 2017 Jan-Carol Publishing

This is a work of fiction. Any resemblance to actual persons, either living or dead is entirely coincidental. All names, characters and events are the product of the author's imagination.

This book may not be reproduced in whole or part, in any manner whatsoever without written permission, with the exception of brief quotations within book reviews or articles.

ISBN: 978-1-945619-26-7
Library of Congress Control Number: 2017943258

You may contact the publisher:
Jan-Carol Publishing, Inc.
PO Box 701
Johnson City, TN 37605
publisher@jancarolpublishing.com
jancarolpublishing.com

*This book is dedicated to all the girls and women who have faced an unplanned pregnancy. Some have had to choose between the baby and the relationship. Some have had to choose adoption or single parenting. No choice was easy. Each choice required courage. You have struggled to do what is best for your baby, And you were compelled by love.
I love you, and I pray for you.*

Dear Reader

I have worked in crisis pregnancy ministry since 1985. None of these stories are true, but many of the conversations are. Mothers who choose to give life are courageous. They sacrifice more than nine months to give life to their babies. They forfeit time, energy, and financial security, rejection by others, and the heartache of living with their choice. If I place my baby for adoption, what will become of her? Will he be loved? Will he forgive me? If I choose to raise my baby, will I deny her a better life? Economic advantage? Parental maturity? A father? God bless those who must choose.

Across America, thousands of ministries serve such women. They are not well-paid, giving sacrificially of their time and talent—and also their finances. But the rewards are eternal. In *Always My Son* we see the social worker, the group therapist, and the housemother pouring their lives out. God bless those who serve.

And God bless you, dear reader, for taking these girls into your heart.

Acknowledgments

I thank all who labor in this vineyard: the professionals who advise us and enable us, the volunteers who donate and give their time, and those who pray. It takes the Body of Christ, working together.

I Killed Your Father

Candy heard someone at the door. Joe must have gotten off early! He tried the handle—strange, he insisted she keep it locked at all times, especially when she was home alone. But he must be as impatient to be off as she was. Finally, they were having their long-delayed honeymoon. She rushed across the living room but hesitated before opening it.

"Joe, is that you?"

"I'm here," a voice answered.

Joe sounds like he has frog in his throat, she thought as she threw it open for his embrace. But this older man wasn't Joe, though he looked like him. Horrified, she slammed the door in his face, but he was too quick and too strong. He jammed his foot into the space and stepped in, closing it behind him.

"And just who are you, you pretty little thing?"

"I'm Candy. We weren't expecting anyone. Perhaps you have the wrong door?"

"Oh, no, sweetheart, I've been scoping this place for days. I know Martha Long lives here, but she won't walk out of this place tonight. I finish what I start, and I should've killed that lying woman *years* ago. She cost me seven years of my life. Who are you and what are you doing here?"

"I'm Joe's wife."

"Whadaya you know. He scored big time. Didn't know he had it in him. Is it good for you, Sweetheart? Because I'm more of a man than he'll ever be." The powerful man stepped closer, twirling a piece of hair in his rough hand. He hadn't bathed, and she smelled his sweat and grime. "But we'll get to that later. I've been in the big house a long time. I got need of a woman."

His hair was black, like Joe's, but streaked with grey and greasy. Joe was fastidious, his hair always immaculately groomed. He never wore dirty clothes, like this man's ragged jeans and slovenly tee shirt of indeterminate color. But Candy knew his type. She had survived many years with her own abuser. Thinking quickly, she began to make a plan.

"Been a while, has it?" she asked, trying to muddle his thoughts. "Let me get you some coffee. It's cold out there." *Think, Candy, think! He'll kill Martha. You fool, Joe has told you over and over never to let anyone in. God help me.* She moved quietly toward the small kitchen in the tidy apartment. *Please let Eddie stay asleep! Spare my baby.*

"I made a fresh pot a while ago," she said, moving quietly but calmly. "Do you like cream, sugar? Have a seat." Apparently, he thought she hadn't heard his threats or that she was taken with his good looks, because he sat, nervously fidgeting with his hands. *I wonder if he he would taste my pain pills in the coffee.*

Candy had refused the pain medication she'd received after having a C-section six weeks ago—after living with Myra at Hope House, she was terrified of the stuff. But she couldn't get to it, because it was in the bedroom she shared with Joe and the baby. *God, help me. I've got to stop him before he kills Martha and Joe.*

"And don't you go putting nothin' in that coffee. You'll drink it first."

Candy clattered the mugs and the spoon. "I'll let you put in your own cream and sugar." She reached for the powered creamer and the sugar bag and behind it to the revolver Joe had taught her to use. She slipped it into the side pocket of her cargo pants leg pocket and walked calmly into the living room, her heart beating so loudly she thought he'd hear it. She set the mug gently on the table beside him—she knew not to rile a man like this.

"Good girl. You know how to please a man, doncha, Sweetheart? Too bad we don't have more time, but Martha should be here any minute. I know. I've watched."

"Uh, she's planning to do some Christmas shopping this afternoon," Candy lied. "She won't be home for a long time."

Before she could duck, his fist connected with her jaw. "You're a liar. Just like a woman," he snarled.

Candy tentatively touched her face, remembering the feel of blows, and the familiar loathing of an abusive male. Reeling from the blow, the weight of the revolver pressed against her leg.

"Never again, Baby, never again will you be helpless before a man, no matter how big or how powerful. I'll teach you how to protect yourself," Joe had said, time after time, when he took her to the shooting range. She hadn't wanted to go, but now she was glad she had. She'd learned her lessons, and she could shoot well. *God, give me a chance, one chance. Martha finally has a life. She loves little Eddie. She deserves a life.*

"Why do you want to hurt Martha?" Candy tried another tactic.

Wrong move. Joe's father stood, his eyes narrowing. "Don't you try nothing if you want to live through this night. She's dead. No woman gets the best of me." He pulled a large gun out of his belt. Curse words tumbled out of his mouth like crumbs spewing out of the lips of an overstuffed child. In his rage, he didn't hear the key, but Candy was listening for it.

"Get away from the door!" she screamed.

Bullets raked the door, leaving holes across about chest level. He was shooting to kill.

Candy grabbed the revolver out of her pocket and pointed it at him as he whirled to face her.

"I saved one for you, you..." but she fired seconds before he got off his last shot. Her first bullet hit his chest, and frothy blood bubbled, but she didn't stop. She shot again, and again, even as he dropped. She stood over him and looked down. His glazed eyes stared at her, but the face she saw was Lester's, and she calmly placed her last bullet through his forehead before collapsing onto the floor.

She didn't hear the screaming, the police order to open the door, Martha's weeping, or Eddie's shrieking.

Martha hovered behind the police. Her eyes swept over the bloody bodies, but she pushed past everyone to get to the bedroom and pick up the terrified baby. Maybe he wasn't her biological grandson, but he was the grandson of her heart. With tears pouring down her cheeks, she brought him to her chest, rubbing his tiny back and swaying.

An officer came to the bedroom door. "The man is dead, but the little lady is alive. The EMTs are on their way. Can you identify them?"

Holding Eddie against her shoulder so he wouldn't see his mother, Martha forced her quivering legs to walk into the front room. "The man is Scooter Long, my ex-husband. He was in prison, and they were supposed to notify me before his release. The world is better without him, but the girl..." Tears rolled across Martha's cheeks and dripped off her chin. "The girl is my daughter-in-law, and the world needs her. Her baby needs her. My son needs her. God, please."

"You'd better call your son, Ma'am. We'll take her to the trauma center at Wexner."

Joe crashed through the open doorway. He'd followed the ambulance and watched, horrified, as it stopped in front of their apartment house. He fell to his knees in front of Candy and drew her bloody body against his chest, keening in his grief.

"Step aside, son," said the older officer. "She's still alive, and we want to make sure she stays that way. We're putting pressure on her thigh where she was shot. Let the EMTs do their job. You can ride in the ambulance, but you have to keep out of our way." Then he lifted Joe to his feet and drew him aside while the other officer maintained pressure on her leg.

Seeing his mother, he said, "What happened?"

Still swaying side to side and making little circles on Eddie's back, she pointed. Joe saw the body of his dead father, being tagged by the police.

"He's dead?" he asked.

"Quite."

"I'm sure it was self-defense," he said.

"Obviously, but he was after someone else first." The young cop pointed to the door, where EMTs poured in.

"Mom, are you okay?" Although concern edged his voice, his eyes never left Candy and the men who were working on her.

One lifted his stethoscope and said, "Strong heartbeat, but the blood loss will take its toll. Get that line in."

Eddie's soft whimpers wrenched Joe's heart, and he stood to move toward where his mother held him. He patted the baby's back, this infant he'd claimed as his own, though he wasn't his flesh and blood.

"She screamed for me to move away from the door when she heard the key, and then I heard the shooting," his mother told him.

The emergency crew had lifted Candy onto a litter. Joe dropped a kiss on Eddie's forehead and gave his mom a quick hug. "Take care of him, Mom," he choked.

"She'll make it, Joey. She'll come home."

Giving a quick nod, Joe followed closely behind the men. "I'll let you know how she is."

The EMTs pointed to a seat as they worked on Candy. One was patched to the hospital and relayed information as he received orders. They moved quickly, putting in an IV and administering something. They asked if he knew her blood type, and he told them he thought it was AB positive, but she'd had a C-section at Doctors General last month, and they'd cross matched her. All the information was quickly transmitted, and the ambulance crew never stopped working on her.

Joe focused on Candy, heedless of the tears coursing down his face. He whispered, "God, please," over and over. When the ambulance screeched into the hospital driveway, he followed the unspoken point and hopped out, turning to watch his wife being lifted out and rushed into the emergency room, where two doctors greeted them.

"We're taking her up to surgery, stat," the older one said. "Follow us."

"You can wait outside—you her husband?" the younger one said, pointing to a chair outside the surgery suite. Joe jerked his head in agreement. The younger surgeon patted his shoulder. "Dr. Jamison happened to be here today. He's the finest vascular surgeon in the country. He'll fix her up."

Joe didn't trust his voice to answer. He turned and saw John, the counselor from Hope House, approaching. Wordlessly, the therapist took him in his arms as he broke down in sobs.

"I never made love to my wife," Joe cried.

"You will. She's going to make it. We've activated the prayer circle. She's young and healthy."

"She's barely recovered from the C-section, John." He raised his head. "What about the hotel reservations? All that money... Everyone was so generous, and it's wasted."

"You let us worry about that. I'll call Beth. Come on over here, and let's pray." John led Joe over to the brown plastic sofa, and they sat together with heads bowed. Joe knew Candy was not in Dr. Jamison's capable hands, she was in her Father's embrace and her surgeon's hands were covered with His. He took a shuddering breath.

"She saved Mom's life," he said, looking up at John.

"That's what Martha said."

"My father's dead. They were supposed to tell us when he was released, but we won't be afraid anymore."

Beth, the social worker from Hope House, and her husband, Tom, were in and out to be with him during the waiting. Even the housemother, Miss Ginny, came by. Hope House had included Joe and Martha in their loving circle. Joe met Candy when she was a resident of the maternity home, and they married there. Joe knew Laura, Cathy, and her mother, Michelle, and even far-away Missy O'Malley in West Virginia, were interceding. Her friends from Hope House remained close. He swiped his hand across his eyes, and John placed a hand on his knee. They looked up as the door to the surgical suite swung open.

Dr. Jamison walked over to them, pulling his surgical cap off his head as he walked. A smile creased his face. "She did very well. We've repaired the artery, and baring complications, she should be fine. She's young and healthy. You can see her in intensive care—oh, go on into recovery." He waved his hand. "Through those double doors, and she's on the right."

Joe felt the elephant's foot lift off his chest as he gazed down at Candy. She had bruises on her face, IVs running in her arm, and lay still, but her chest rose quietly, steadily, up and down. The monitors blinked and beeped in even rhythm.

A nurse patted his arm. "She's stable and doing well. We'll monitor her until the anesthesia wears off, and send her to intensive care." Seeing the alarm on his face, she added, "It's routine for this kind of surgery— as a precaution."

"When will she be in a regular room? Can I see her?" Joe took her limp hand and brought it up to his lips. He leaned and whispered, "Hey, Girl, you keep fighting, Baby. I love you."

A shadow of a smile crossed Candy's face and a small sigh escaped her lips. "I'll make sure you do," the nurse said. "You're good for her." But she gestured for him to go, and he reluctantly obeyed.

Joe hated hospitals. He'd taken his mother too many times, lied too often, but the man who caused all the pain and lies was gone. Thank God.

He realized he needed to contact his mother, and pushed her number the minute he reached the waiting area. He learned John had already called to report Candy was out of surgery, but Martha was happy to hear that Joe had seen her, and told him Eddie was fine. Since they'd planned for their honeymoon trip, Candy had stored several bottles of milk.

"Don't worry about Eddie, Joe. Just take care of her and bring her home."

"They'll have her in critical care for a while, but the doctor says if all goes well, she'll be home in two weeks."

"It will—so many people are praying."

"I love her so much, Mom."

"I know you do, and she loves you, too. Your love has made her strong."

"What will this do to her?"

Martha sucked in a breath. "God will help her, and we'll be there for her."

"John is here. He never left my side." Joe looked up at the psychologist gratefully.

"God with skin on," John murmured his oft-repeated phrase when Joe hung up, and he put his arm around the young man's shoulder.

"I'm okay, John. Go on home to your family."

"Someone will be here soon," he said.

Michelle walked in and silently took his hand, and so it was for the hours they stood watch. Cathy and her mom, and Miss Ginny took shifts during the long hours until she was moved to a regular room. Joe was allowed in critical care, and his was the first face she saw when she woke.

He whispered her name, holding her hand, and her smoky grey eyes opened.

"Hey, Beautiful," he said.

"Hey yourself." She smiled.

"I love you."

"Back at you." She closed her eyes and winced.

"Need something for pain?"

"No. I killed him, Joe. I killed your father."

"You killed a monster, and saved Mom's life."

"Thank God. Is she okay? She didn't get hit?"

"She's fine. She heard your warning and got out of the way."

"She's taking care of Eddie?"

"Of course she's with Eddie. Don't worry about a thing. You rest."

A nurse had noticed her return to consciousness on the monitors, and came in to check on her. "You'll be in a regular room soon, at this rate."

"I need a breast pump," Candy said.

"The baby can't use this milk with all the meds you are on, but you do need to keep your supply if you intend to continue nursing. I'll go get that." She patted Candy's hand and pointed Joe to the door. He kissed Candy's forehead, squeezed her hand, and reluctantly left.

The First Time I Saw You

Joe told Candy not to worry about Eddie, but the next day she refused pain meds and fretted about pumping her breasts. The breast pump eased her anxiety somewhat, but the effort wore her out. While she slept, Joe watched her, remembering the first time he saw her when she came to the GED class. She looked rugged then—bleached white hair with dark roots, garish make-up, and absolutely no clue about the subjects. She didn't even try to get the answers, and shrugged when asked for them. Joe had been a Christian for five years at that time, and girls who looked cheap didn't appeal to him—but something about Candy grabbed him. Later he realized the hesitant, haunted fear surrounding an abused woman. She put him in mind of his own mother. He offered to help her, but she looked startled and refused. So it continued, until one Monday morning when she arrived at class with all her math homework complete and a clear command of the assignment.

"Good job, Candy," Joe said at break. "You got this cold."

"We have a new girl at Hope House—you know I live there, right?—Missy O'Malley. She's sweet and smart, and she helped me. She made it really easy."

"No, I didn't know you lived there, but you come with Michelle. Are you both..."

"Pregnant? Yeah, I'm due in October, and she's due in January."

Joe tried to read her expression as she turned away to avoid his response. He thought she expected his contempt, but he felt compassion. She looked young, and not nearly as hard as her dark roots proclaimed. He wondered what her story was, but she picked up her books and moved across the room, holding them tightly against her chest. He tried to put her out of his mind. He had enough problems of his own, after all, trying to work and get his GED so he could get his electrician's certificate. He and his mom had fled Kentucky five years ago, after the trial that landed his father in the state penitentiary. The last beating had left his mother near death, and the hospital called in protective services. He was in a foster home until she was released. Once she returned home, she swallowed her pride and accepted food stamps, trying to get a job to support them, but she had no skills.

After the trial, they moved to Columbus, Ohio, so she could find a job in the city and start over; Joe insisted he'd drop out of school and work. He knew his mom couldn't support them by herself. After a few years, they had a nicer apartment, and his mom had a job in a dry-cleaning place, where she tended the register and made alterations. She was a good seamstress, so she bought a sewing machine and took classes. Joe took a night job and attended GED classes.

"Mr. Long, are you with us?" The teacher's voice had intruded on Joe's wandering thoughts.

"Pardon me, Ma'am, I guess I was half-asleep. Could you repeat the question?"

Candy caught his eye, with a sympathetic glance. Grammar was not easy for either of them, because they had both come from rural areas and struggled with dialects—hers Southern, and his Appalachian.

After Joe flubbed the question miserably and the teacher asked if he had even studied the lesson, class was dismissed. He gathered his books together and bolted for the door, head down.

"Wait up, Joe." Surprised, he saw Candy approaching "This grammar stuff is hard for me, too," she said. "My friend is helping me this afternoon. Do you want to stop by?" He hesitated. "You could take my bus. That is, if you want. Missy's real good with grammar. Her grandmother was an English teacher. She's from West Virginia, but she talks real good."

Michelle joined them, adding her encouragement. Joe usually napped before going to his night watchman job, but he shrugged and followed them to the bus. They got off at the corner and walked to the beautiful house that housed six pregnant girls.

"Mrs. G, we brought home a classmate. Can we have another plate?" Michelle asked when they opened the back door and stepped into a warm kitchen. The smell of cookies hit his nose, and he grinned.

After introductions, the housemother set out another plate of chocolate chip cookies and added a glass of milk. Other girls piled into the kitchen, excitedly chattering. Joe was uncomfortable. Cathy was quite pregnant, and recently she'd started homebound instruction. Missy showed, but she was going to attend regular school when it opened the next week; Myra, Candy's roommate, had skipped GED classes today. Of all the girls, Joe liked Missy and Michelle the best-but he remained sympathetic toward Candy.

Missy settled Candy and Joe at the dining room table, drawing their assignments in front of her to look them over "This looks easy, let's get to it." That afternoon Joe finally understood nouns, pronouns, and verbs, and their cases and tenses.

"But you said nouns are subjects and objects. If verbs can't be subjects, what about 'Swimming is my favorite sport?' Swimming is the subject of the sentence. Isn't swimming a verb?" Joe asked.

Candy looked confused and looked at Missy with a question in her eyes.

Missy laughed—she had a great laugh. "Good question, Joe!" She gave his shoulder a light punch and then explained gerunds, the ing-verbs that acted as nouns.

"That's too much!" Joe moaned. "I'll never get this."

"Sure you will, Joe. You recognized the subject of the sentence. You've learned a lot in one afternoon," Missy encouraged.

"I'd best be going now, thanks. I have a night job, and I need to cook for Mom before I go."

Beth, the social worker for Hope House, came into the dining room and met Joe. She offered him a ride, saying she was on her way home.

Joe, usually shy, found himself accepting. He liked these kind folks, recognizing they were fellow Christians. When Beth cranked her car, a Christian radio station came on, and Joe identified the singing group, one of his favorites.

"I thought you were a Christian," Beth commented when he knew the song and the musicians, and asked him where they went to church. "Hope House is a Christian ministry, but not all the girls are Christians—yet!" Her eyes twinkled. "Our goal is to love them all to Jesus."

"Missy is a Christian, I can tell," Joe said.

"She is—and pregnant through no fault of her own, but bearing her circumstances like an overcomer and ministering to all the girls around her. Her roommate, Cathy, is a new believer, and she has grown by leaps and bounds since Missy came."

Joe wanted to ask about Candy, but figured he should ask her himself. When Beth dropped him off, he thanked her for getting him home in time to fix dinner. He hopped out of the car with a wave.

"Whatcha thinking, Joe?" Candy's voice startled him out of his memories.

"I was thinking about when we met, and the day I came to Hope House the first time."

"I was pretty rough back then, but you were always kind to me. Some of the guys were mean, but you were a perfect gentleman and always showed a Christian attitude to us Hope House girls."

"I was drawn to you from the first—I recognized something underneath your toughness."

"What was that?"

Joe leaned over the bed and pushed his wife's soft brown hair off her forehead. "I dunno—I think I recognized the haunted look I saw on Mom's face. I knew you'd been through some tough times."

"I remember when I told you how I got pregnant, and you said, 'I knew it was something like that.' You almost cried."

"I could tell the day you got saved. You walked into class, and I saw it in your eyes."

"Missy O'Malley changed my life. The next week, she cooked up that plan for Michelle and me to have make-overs."

"Your outside matched the new creation."

"I remember when you told me I'd have to forgive Lester. Man, I was furious with you. You'd never been a helpless girl raped night after night by an abuser."

"I had no right to say that. I'm sorry."

"But it was true. I got no peace until I turned him over to God."

"Have I ever told you how proud I am of you?" Joe asked.

Candy reached over and entwined her fingers in his. "You've been patient. Your love has given me strength to do the impossible—you and John."

John Morgan popped his head in the room. "You're awake and looking much better. I went to ICU and found out you were in a regular room. Good job. How are you doing? And not just physically." John crossed the room and took Candy's hand but glanced at Joe. "The police asked if they could interview you today," he said to Candy. "Are you ready for that?"

"I killed him, John, and, God forgive me, I'm not sorry."

"He almost killed Martha, and he tried to kill you," John said.

Candy's smoky eyes filled—John had seen them spill over many, many times in the months he'd known her. "I know, but I still killed another human being. Jesus forgives me. He's been really close to me in the hospital."

"That's good. Let's ask Him to help you with these questions."

As they finished praying, a knock sounded. Joe squeezed her hand and watched her face as John pulled the door open and two men in uniform stepped in. Joe thought he recognized them, but he'd been beside himself with fear several days ago.

Candy caught her breath.

"You're looking good, Mrs. Long. How's our brave hero doing today?" One of the policemen said. "I'm sure you don't remember me. I'm Officer Rodriguez, Mario Rodriguez, and this here's Abe Miller."

The younger man stretched his hand to shake Joe's. "I guess this has been a long couple of days for you."

"I killed him," Candy said.

"And you did a good job," the older man said. "Martha told us you warned her, and she hit the floor. The bullet holes were right where she would've been standing. Good thinking—but it cost you, didn't it? I need to know why you had a gun. Martha says you have a concealed carry permit, but we need to find it."

"It's in the drawer in my nightstand," Joe said.

"Mind if we get it and record the number?"

"No problem."

"Do I need a lawyer?" Candy asked, her eyes wide.

The cop grinned. "You need an agent. No charges. You're the hero of Ohio and Kentucky. He killed three cops when he escaped. Killed one with his bare hands, got his gun, and shot two others. We cops don't like those who kill our own. You did an amazing thing, kept your head, and took him out before your mother-in-law was his next victim. You're a brave woman, Mrs. Long. Because of your warning, she dove to the side and wasn't injured. All of Columbus has been praying for you, Ma'am."

Joe thought his heart would break when Candy wept. "I didn't have any choice—he planned to rape me, and then I'd be next. I've been..." her voice trailed off, but Joe knew the rest of the sentence: she'd been raped enough.

She looked at Joe and said, "I stood over him. He might have been dead already, but I saw his face, and it was Lester's. I put a bullet straight between his eyes."

She shuddered, breaking into sobs, and Joe gathered her into his arms, whispering, "Shh."

"He was killed on the first shot. You got him right in the heart, good as our sniper would have done. Where'd you learn to shoot like that?"

Keeping his arms around her, Joe explained, "I bought the gun and took her to the shooting range. She'd been abused by her mother's boyfriend for years, and he wasn't jailed because he denied her charges. He didn't want her testimony, and I figured she needed to be able to defend herself when I wasn't home. When the baby was born, the DNA proved she was right. She was a minor, and now he's in jail. Two little kids from the neighborhood testified he had molested them, too."

The older officer gave a short laugh. "I don't envy his chances in the pen—inmates don't care for child molesters."

"So the kid isn't yours?" Abe asked.

Joe's eyes flared. "The baby will always be mine. He's my son."

"He's one lucky kid then," the younger officer said.

The older officer looked at him with respect. "She's doing okay"?"

"Yeah." Joe kept his arms around Candy, and gathered her close as she quietly wept.

"Look, we don't need any more. I'll get that concealed carry permit, and we'll tie up this report." Officer Rodriguez stood. "Once again, thanks for what you did, Mrs. Long. You removed an evil from the streets."

"I don't have to go to jail?"

"Are you kidding me? No, Ma'am; you don't even have to go to trial. The mayor wants to give you a citizen's medal for bravery, as soon as you're up to it."

A nurse hovering in the corner stepped forward. She poured cool water on a washcloth and stood ready to place it over Candy's swollen eyes.

"One more thing—where did you get the fat lip?" Rodriguez asked.

"He knew I was lying about when Mom would be home, and he punched me."

"A murderer and a scumbag!" Abe Miller said. He patted her awkwardly on her shoulder. "Hope you feel better soon."

The officers moved to the doorway, but Rodriguez looked back. "You might want to turn to channel six. We'll be having a press conference in ten minutes."

"How are you doing, Candy?" John asked when they left.

"Not too bad. I'm relieved I won't face trial, but it was hard talking about it. I never thought I'd kill another human being."

Joe had perched on the side of her bed so he could keep his arms around her. She rested her head back against his chest.

"Even when I wanted Lester to die, I dreamed he'd get killed driving drunk, or someone else would kill him in a bar fight. I never planned to do that."

John scooted his chair closer to the bed and took her hand. "Of course you didn't, Candy. Only a very sick man like Scooter Long plans to kill someone. Your baby was in the other room. Martha was at the door. You did what you had to do, to protect them."

"Is this how a soldier feels in war? It's kill or be killed. I tried to talk him out of it, but when I said Martha was a good person, he cussed her and screamed at me. It distracted him from hearing her key, and I could cry out. He was facing me, so he had to swing around to shoot at the door."

"That's what gave her time to get out of the way. You saved Mom's life."

"Your mom's been like a mother to me."

"She loves you, too. You're the daughter she always wanted."

"Let's turn on the TV," Candy said.

"You don't have to watch," John told her.

"We can turn it off if it gets ugly," she replied.

Joe picked up the remote, and they saw a crowded room. A door opened to the side and the two officers and several doctors stepped in. First, the medical professionals gave an overview of her condition and her injuries, and how they'd repaired them.

One reporter asked if she had been critically injured, and the doctor told him if the EMTs hadn't done everything they did, she would have died before she got to the hospital.

"It was touch and go in surgery, and we thought we'd lost her at one point, but she's a strong lady. Yes, it was a critical injury. The femoral artery was damaged, and we had to put in a vein graft. If her neighbor hadn't called 911 immediately, and if that patrol car hadn't been in the immediate vicinity, she wouldn't be here today. Those officers knew what to do, and they did their job well."

Joe's arms tightened around his wife and his lips brushed her hair. "Thank you, God!"

In response to another question, the doctor added, "She's responding well. She's sitting up and eating, and she should live a normal life."

Another doctor stepped up to the bank of microphones. "I'd like to add that much of her miracle is due to the devotion of her husband. This young man never left her side, and he called her back to life. In situations like this, we surgeons know we're only a part of the miracle of life."

The doctors left and the policemen took their place, reviewing what they could about the details of the investigation. No charges were filed, as it was obviously self-defense. They praised Candy's quick thinking and excellent gunmanship, crediting her with stopping untold carnage, and went on to describe the deaths of three policemen in Kentucky during his escape.

Hands shot up in the air, and they detailed as much as they could, finally turning it over to the mayor.

"As soon as Candy is able, we plan to present her a citation and a citizen's medal for bravery," he announced. "We'll make you aware of the time and place, gentlemen and ladies, and for now, good-day."

Joe felt Candy leaning heavier against him. He brushed his lips on her forehead and asked if she was ready to lie down. At her nod, he eased her onto the pillow. "Do you need something to sleep?" he asked.

"I'm good," she whispered and closed her eyes.

Joe looked up at John. "Others are only recognizing what I've known a long time. She's one of the strongest, best people I've ever known."

"In a strange way, this may be a good thing for her," John said. "She will have affirmation of her worth, of her courage and resilience. It has been a privilege to work with her—and with you, Joe. God certainly gave you and your love to her."

"I'm the lucky one, John."

"She might argue with you on that one. You get some rest now, while she sleeps." The therapist stood. "In fact, maybe you should go home awhile."

Joe shook his head.

"The hospital psychiatrist will be in this afternoon—it's protocol in situations like this. He's a nice guy. I've worked with him before, and we ran into each other in the hall yesterday. He didn't come in then because I told him I had been with her at Hope House. Get some sleep, Joe."

And Joe did. Although he and Candy had not spoken of it, they both had worried about an investigation and a trial, and that fear had been removed today.

The Hope House Family

Candy grinned when Cathy pushed the door open. "The nurse warned me that I can't stay long, but since you're awake and eating lunch, I could come in." The Hope House girls were more than friends. Cathy took Candy into her arms.

"Hey, Girlfriend. How're you feeling?"

"I want to go home and see Eddie."

"I just left the apartment. He's doing great, and Martha's bringing him in this afternoon."

Candy patted the edge of the bed, and Cathy perched on it.

"How are Stanley and your mom?"

"We're doing good. Last night, we watched a movie, and laughed and cried. Mom's not like I thought she was—I guess she's growing stronger. Beth helped her fight for alimony, and now she's going to school, learning medical billing. I'll stay home with the baby until she's done, and we'll figure out watching him when I go back to school. It's great having a real mom." Cathy stopped abruptly. "Oh, I'm sorry, Candy."

"Martha's my real mom, Cath. It's okay."

"We've come a long way since that first week at Hope House. Remember how we tried to out-do each other with horrible mother stories? Now we both have real moms. Thank You, Jesus!"

Candy, a ward of the state, had arrived at Hope House after Cathy, whose parents granted custody to Hope House. They shared bitterness toward the mothers they felt had failed them, and they had, but through the grace of God, the girls had worked through some measure of forgiveness. With John's help, Cathy had reconciled with her mother, and they now shared an apartment. Candy's mother, on the other hand, continued to stand by her man throughout his trial, and Candy had no support until Joe's mother came into her life.

"You shamed me when I was complaining about Mom, and you said at least she'd never slapped me and accused me of taking her husband, or cussed me," Cathy said. "She hadn't done anything like that, but she was a doormat. She never said anything. That's why I ran away. Daddy wasn't going to do me that way. Now I know Mom was an emotionally abused woman herself. When they found me, she stood up to my father for the first time, and he dumped her. He got himself another wife he could walk all over. Mom's getting stronger. I'm proud of her."

"Remember when John led that Bible study on forgiveness?" Cathy asked. "Pastor had preached the sermon on the debtor who refused to forgive his fellow servant, and the Holy Spirit had been working on me all week. Then John challenged us to forgive those who have hurt us."

"Yeah, and I thought I had to make peace with Lester," Candy shuddered. "Joe had already told me I needed to forgive him, and I was furious!"

"John explained you didn't need a relationship with an abuser, but you needed to let go so he couldn't hurt you anymore."

"That was a relief! And Joe was right—when I turned him over to God, I was free."

"I, on the other hand, had to face my mom, you bum! And you had this hunky guy who adored you."

Candy giggled. "He did *not* adore me at the time. He was a friend."

"Yeah, but as soon as you and Michelle got your makeovers, he was drooling all over you."

Candy pushed her friend. "Stop!"

"Where is Joe? Martha told me he never leaves your side."

"He's gone for a walk. He knew you were coming, and he decided to stretch his legs while you're here."

"'Chelle told me when you went to class the next day he couldn't keep his eyes off you."

"We started preparing for the exam together, and it was hard to concentrate." Candy laughed again, putting her hands up to her blushing face.

"John asked you about your 'relationship' with this young man, and you said—"

"I don't have no relationship, John, he's a friend."

"And John said, 'Friendship is a relationship, Candy, and the best way to begin a romance.' Ooh, did you blush!"

"And Missy said, 'That was a double negative, Candy!' and we all laughed."

"Then Mrs. G suggested we invite him to dinner, and all of you hung over me when I made the call," Candy remembered.

"Poor guy, he had all of us making sure he was good enough for our friend. Maybe we didn't have families behind us, but we had each other's backs!" Cathy said.

"Gosh, I love you guys!" Candy held her arms out and the girls clung to one another.

"We love you, too." Cathy looked up at the nurse who came in to check on her patient, and pulled away. "I'm sorry. I'd better get out of here."

"You've been good for her. I heard you giggle. But her baby is coming in this afternoon, and she needs her strength." Cathy gave her friend a final hug and left.

"Joe's in the hall, Candy, talking to his mom." The nurse took Candy's blood pressure and checked her pulse. She patted her hand before taking her to the bathroom. When they came back into the room, Joe sat, his head in his hands, and Candy knew he was praying.

"What is it, Joe?" she asked with alarm. "Is Eddie all right?"

Joe stood and took her into his arms. She was standing, and it was their first real embrace since the surgery. "He's fine, and Mom's bringing him over soon. It's... We got some news."

"What?"

"Lester's dead."

"How?"

"Officer Rodriguez was right—other inmates don't like child molesters. A bunch of them jumped him with a prison-made knife."

She shuddered and took a breath. "I guess this means we're both really free—that is, if my mom doesn't come after me." She gave a shaky laugh.

"Your mom's in the hospital, Candy. They think it might be bronchitis or something worse."

Joe helped her to the bed, and she sat, leaning her head against him. "God help her. She smoked two packs a day. I bet she has cancer."

"Could be. Mom said she got two calls, one from the prison and one from your counselor at school."

"She believed me, Joe, when I told her what had been going on at home. I never had to go back, not one more night. In fact, I went home with her. She called in social services."

"You told me your face was pretty black and blue that day."

"Mom slapped me around after Lester had already blacked my eye. Mrs. Wanless saw me come in the door and took me straight to her office. 'I'm not letting you brush this off, Candy. Now you give it to me, and give it to me straight,' she said. I broke down and cried for two hours. I couldn't believe she thought I was telling the truth. She said she knew something was going on. I had good grades until he started…"

Joe lifted her legs into bed and settled pillows around her. "Mom wanted to make sure you could handle all this before she brought the baby in."

"I need my baby, Joe."

"I know you do—I could use a daddy-fix myself." Candy's grey eyes filled. "What? What's with the tears, Baby?"

"I love you, Joe. I love the way you love Eddie."

He pulled the sheet up around her and brushed his lips on hers. "I told Mom to come on unless I called, but I figured you'd be relieved—about Lester, I mean, not about your mother."

"I should feel something for her, I guess, but I just feel…flat. I feel flat. She never called me after the trial; I was sure she'd call to say she was sorry."

"I was glad they took a deposition from here and didn't make you go. They had the tapes of the original interview. When the DNA came up with a match, he couldn't lie any longer. I'm glad you didn't have to go."

"The doctors didn't want me to make the trip after the C-section. I think John talked to the judge, too." Candy leaned back, weary with emotional overload. She closed her eyes, but roused when she heard Eddie cooing. She raised her bed with a smile.

Joe winked at her. "I'll bring him in."

Eddie stared at the only father he'd ever known, searching his face as if to ask where he'd been. Joe snuggled with him, sweet-talking him and smiling. "I swear he's grown in three days! I love you, Boy." Joe spread kisses over his face and tummy.

"Give me my baby, Joe."

Joe cuddled him, teasing her briefly by holding Eddie out of her reach before he settled him in her arms.

Eddie immediately began nuzzling, and Candy beamed. "I thought he'd forget me." She lowered her gown, and he latched on, pulling deeply. Mommy felt sweet relief—she been using the pump, but nothing was like her babe at her breast.

Joe watched the two of them and sat down beside them on the edge of the bed. "When we get you out of here—as soon as they let us—and we can go on our trip, let's take him with us."

"You want to take Eddie on our honeymoon?"

"Yeah, I do. Do you mind?"

"I never wanted to leave him, but I thought you deserved to be first."

"I didn't want to leave him either. You always came as a package deal—you and Eddie. We'll order a crib for the room, then. Deal?"

"Deal. Gosh, Joe, I don't believe you're real."

He stroked her cheek with the back of his hand, and Eddie looked up. "Hey, Baby, ready for the other side? Mommy has needed you in the worst way." He helped her shift him. When the baby had finished, Joe put him over his shoulder to burp him, and opened the door to admit his mother.

"He did okay with the bottle, but I had to convince him every time," Martha said as she bustled in and took note of his bulging tummy. "Hey, Little Pig," she said, but his eyes closed and he slept.

"Has he been fussy?" Candy asked.

"He's a good baby, but he hasn't been himself. He'd only eat a little bit at a time, and I knew it was only because he was hungry. He missed his mama."

"Thank you, Mom. Candy knew he'd be fine with you."

"What about your job?" Candy asked.

"So far, so good. It's all over the news, and they've been nice about it. Lots of people have sent donations and gifts. He won't need toys for the next five years!" Martha said.

"Columbus is a nice town," Candy said.

"Oh, Honey, you're a household name. These things have come from all over the country. And the NRA called. They want you to be a spokesperson. They said they'd pay you to make some spots."

"We need the money, but I'd definitely have to pray about that."

"That's what I told them."

Joe was sitting in the chair with one leg across his other knee and the baby on his shoulder when Candy's doctor came in.

"So, this is the famous baby?" He walked over to Joe and smiled when Joe lowered him in his arms.

He winked at Candy. "He's worth getting well for, isn't he, Mom?"

"You bet!"

"You're doing well enough to go home the end of the week, if you stay in bed for another week. Then, if all is well, we can get the two of you off on this trip you have planned, right?" He grinned.

"We decided it would be the three of us. We're taking the baby," Joe said.

The doctor looked surprised. "You're an amazing guy, Joe Long."

"Isn't he?" Candy agreed, reaching her hand across the bed to take Joe's.

"All right, we'll shoot for Thursday or Friday if we can get up you and walking more today and tomorrow. The mayor wants to do another press conference and the citation before you leave the hospital." He walked to the door, but turned back. "It's been an honor working with you two. It has renewed my faith in God and man."

As soon as they heard his footsteps go down the hall, they began to pray for him. The nurse pulled in another chair for Joe's mother, and the family visited with lighter hearts that afternoon. Eddie nursed frequently, and Martha helped Candy walk a bit.

After the nurse put Candy back in bed, she told Martha she'd bring in the bottles they'd stored. "I know you want to get home to nurse him, Candy, but that's good for a start."

Mrs. G, the housemother from Hope House, arrived. She planned to visit and take Martha home. "Michelle wanted to come, but I knew Eddie would be here, and I thought it would be better for her to come another time."

"How's she doing, Mrs. G?"

"Very well. She is sure of her decision, and the baby's parents are lovely people. She has started back at the college, and she's moved in with an older couple from her church. They have grown children who live away, and they're thrilled to have someone in the house. Michelle will be fine, Candy. Laura's coming to see you—and I think Missy is, too."

"Oh, wow! How did I deserve all this attention?"

"It's not every day someone rescues others and almost dies doing it. You've made national TV," Mrs. G said. "These are your friends, and they love you."

"The Hope House Girls. The closest thing to family I've ever had—until Joe and Martha," Candy said.

"We have new girls at the home now, but the five of you were special. We all rallied around Missy O'Malley, didn't we? She's having a hard time grieving for her Gracie—and apparently, her brother started drinking again."

"Oh, no! I thought he was engaged?" Candy cried, and the gathering went to prayer again. Eddie whimpered, and Joe stood to juggle him. "I don't want you to take him away, but I know you have to. Thank you, Mom. I don't worry, but I miss him."

"I know, Honey. I love you, Sweet Thing." Martha took Candy into her arms. "You'll be home soon, and I'll bring him back tomorrow."

"Meantime, he's about to eat my shirt!" Joe said, laughing and handing him over to Candy.

After Eddie nursed again, Martha wrapped him snugly and followed Ginny out of the room as they all called out, "See you tomorrow."

Candy was tired but happy, and relieved she didn't have to fool with the breast pump. Joe picked up his school books while she leafed through a magazine Ginny had brought, but she couldn't concentrate. She leaned her head back and closed her eyes. Candy was ready to walk when she woke up; Joe took her up and down the halls, amazed at her increasing strength.

"You're determined to get home, aren't you?"

"I am. Do you think he'll let me go to church on Sunday?"

"Who? The doctor? He said rest for a week. Hey, we have a weekend together to store up for, remember?"

She blushed and ducked her head, and he put his arm around her and pulled her close.

Joe's Patience

The next day the Hope House social worker, Beth, brought Martha to the hospital. Joe slipped out of the room, leaving Martha and the baby with Candy. "Beth, can I talk to you a minute?"

"Sure, let's sit in the lobby—or maybe you'd like to go to the cafeteria?"

Joe got a Coke and a sandwich and sat down at a small table, fidgeting a bit.

"What is it, Joe?" Beth asked, putting her hand on his.

He blushed. "I've talked to John—a lot—about Candy, and he's given me some books to read and lots of advice. Marriage is going to be tough for her, and I have to go slow and be gentle. She's...well, you know what's she's been through." Beth nodded. "One night I came into our room and she was bending over the laundry basket. I patted her on her butt—real gentle like—and she jumped up and spun around. I thought she was going to deck me, but she was sorry. She hugged me, and said she didn't know it was me." Joe sipped his Coke and took a bite from his sandwich. "It's gonna be a long road."

"I've talked to her, too, Joe, and she does love you and wants to be a good wife."

"She hasn't read the books you gave her though."

"I'll talk to her some more this week, okay? You'll get through this, Joe, and I'll pray for your patience."

"What I wondered is... I mean, I don't want to push her or anything, and I'll wait as long as it takes, but she wears these sweat pants and baggy shirts all the time—'course she's been pregnant and all, but she doesn't have anything...you know, nice. I know sexy would probably be scary, but could we buy her something pretty?"

"Of course! How thoughtful, Joe. We'll plan a little lingerie shower for her next week Nothing too revealing, but silk pajamas and maybe a nice sleep shirt and a robe. I'll get the girls on it. They want to do something."

"I thought about buying her something myself, but I was afraid she'd think I'm pressuring her."

"You're going to do fine, Joe."

The next morning, the mayor presented Candy a citation and a $10,000 reward before she left the hospital. Her discharge time and date was kept confidential, so she could get home without a lot of fanfare.

Two days after they'd returned home, they had the party. Joe had gone back to school and to work. He was amazed by how nice everyone had been, and he didn't even have to ask for time off. He was given a week, with pay, even after all the family leave time he's taken while she was in the hospital with the C-section.

The girls piled into the apartment, their arms overflowing with boxes and a cake, napkins, punch, and cookies. Beth joined them, stepping over legs to find herself a spot. The apartment was crowded with laughing girls, Cathy, and her mother, Laura, who was living with them, and Michelle. Giggling, they looked around.

"Who's missing?" Michelle asked.

"Martha's in the kitchen. She'll be right out," Candy said.

"I think someone else is missing," Laura said.

Cathy walked to the door and stuck her head out into the hall. "Anybody here?"

Beth knew Missy O'Malley would be the best gift for Candy—they all remembered the day Missy led her to Christ. When she ran into the room, laughing, she pulled Candy into a hug, and Candy screamed.

Missy said, "You look good. On TV at the deal with the mayor, I told Mom you were pale as a ghost."

Martha began distributing paper cups of punch. "She has gotten a lot of color back, hasn't she?"

Cathy's mother offered to help her, and the two older women brought out plates of cake while the Hope House girls chattered. Martha was beside Candy on the couch, and Cathy's mother was on a kitchen chair. Candy patted the other side of the couch, and Beth scooted in. The girls circled together in the small living room.

After refreshments, the girls pushed boxes toward Candy. "Now, open your pretties," Laura insisted.

Candy turned scarlet. "If you guys bought me bad stuff, I'm going to kill you!"

"Oh, we're all jealous because you've got a man, Girl," Cathy said.

"Yeah, and he's a hunk, too," Michelle teased.

Missy leaned forward and took her hand. "The most important thing is, Candy, Joe loves you–and you want to be pretty for him, right?'

Candy looked at her gratefully. "I do. He's a wonderful guy, Missy. You should see him with the baby."

"Speaking of the baby," Martha said, standing and heading for the bedroom. "Go ahead, open up. I'll see everything later. I'll change him."

Beth handed her the first one. Candy took a deep breath and reached for the beautifully wrapped package. She pulled on the ribbon and ripped the paper. She lifted a lid and found a soft plush robe. She rubbed it against her cheek. "This is pretty." Glancing at the card, she thanked Cathy and her mother.

Another box moved across the sea of hands. Candy laughed at slippers with pompoms. "You must have bought these together."

"We did," Laura said. We all went shopping last night."

Michelle said, "This one's from me."

Candy found a modest soft blue night shirt that pulled over her head and went to her knees. "That's nice, too. Everything is really pretty."

"Mine," Missy said, handing up another. "It matches your eyes." Candy lifted out a dove grey pair of silk pajamas. Everyone oohed. "Mom sends her love, Candy."

"I love your mom, Missy."

"I guess this is the last one." Beth lifted her box and put it in Candy's lap.

"I've never worn stuff like this," Candy said, with tears in her eyes.

Martha came out with Eddie on her shoulder. He was snorting and protesting the delay, so Candy quickly unwrapped Beth's gift and lifted out a white eyelet gown, with delicate embroidery. All the girls fingered it.

"It's beautiful, Beth," Michelle said. "Did you do the needlework?"

"Miss Ginny did. She wanted to be here, but the girls are coming home from school."

"We don't have another inch of room in here," Laura said. "But I do miss her."

Cathy's mother stuffed wrapping paper in a garbage bag. "We don't want to wear Candy out, Girls."

"Can we see the baby?" Michelle asked.

Martha handed Eddie over to Candy, and he immediately nuzzled her front. The girls giggled, and Cathy reached for him.

Cathy jiggled the baby on her knee while Candy tugged her tee shirt up and unsnapped the nursing bra. "Gosh he's tiny! I can't believe Stanley was that little a few months ago." Eddie started nuzzling her front, so she handed him back to Candy.

"They are both adorable," Michelle pronounced.

"And he's eating Mommy's shirt!" Missy said.

Soon all the girls laughed at his loud gulping.

Beth urged the girls to leave, and come back one at a time so they wouldn't be too much for her.

"Missy, can you stay? Everyone else is nearby—when do you have to go home?"

"Sunday—I'm staying at Beth's," Missy replied. She stood and hugged everyone, promising to see them over the next few days. She looked at Beth, who agreed they could stay a little longer.

The girls flocked out, and Martha folded each item, exclaiming over them as she carried them into the other room. "Do you want to show them to Joe?"

"I don't think so. Can you put them in a suitcase?"

Beth and Missy visited with Candy while she nursed, and then Missy took the baby to her shoulder, cradling his tiny head against her.

"He's wonderful, Candy. Just precious..." Her voice cracked. "Thank God for Joe; you are blessed. You love that man well, Candy. This is one really blessed baby to have him for a daddy."

The door pushed open and Joe walked in. "Where's my boy?" he asked. He pulled Missy into a hug. "I heard you were coming. How're you doing, Miss?" he chucked Eddie under his chin, and took him into his arms.

"Hey, Joe." Missy hugged her friend tightly. "He's a doll baby."

"He is. He has his mother's beautiful eyes." Joe kissed Candy on the cheek, tugging a lock of her hair. "Gonna show me whatcha got?" he teased.

"Next week."

"Next weekend," he replied. "Hey, Boy." Joe cuddled Eddie into his chest. "You're looking good, Candy. Did you have fun? Are you tired?" He rubbed small circles on the baby's back. "He's a good baby, Missy. He sleeps four hours at a time, now."

Watching Missy blinking back tears, Beth rose. "We've got to get home to feed my kids. You got some lovely things, Candy. I'll be here in the morning, and we'll get to work."

"He usually naps around ten."

Missy hugged her friend one last time. "I'll come by tomorrow."

"Please?" Candy begged.

"You couldn't keep me away." Missy said. "I rode over here with Beth, but I have my car at her house."

Beth and Missy left together. "That is a beautiful pair of pajamas," Beth said, "It does match her eyes. Everyone chose well."

"I've been doubling up on my prayers for Candy and Joe, even before the shooting. I know they haven't been...you know, *together*. Joe's been really patient, and this is going to be hard for her. I can't imagine." She shuddered. "I want to get married and have a family, but I'm not even interested in dating right now. I only experienced violence one night, and Candy suffered for years. And when my mom found out, she took me in her lap, big as I am, and rocked me. I can still her whispering, 'Shh, baby, we'll get through this. Mama's here.' Candy's mother slapped her face and didn't believe her!"

Stopping at a red light, Beth reached over and squeezed Missy's hand.

"I don't want to ever, you know, have sex. Maybe I won't get married. Candy said one time she went to the health department and had an exam. She was red and chapped, so the nurse gave her some Vaseline in a tube. That horrible man got all excited when she used it. He said he knew she's learn to like it, and maybe now she'd quit fighting him. She told him she didn't like it and she wanted him to quit." Tears began to trickle down Missy's cheeks. "You know what he did? He bit her, hard, on her boob."

"You've described a rape, an act of violence. Joe loves her. He'll be gentle. Making love with someone you love is a wonderful experience."

"I guess, but I don't see it. Candy went into gym class the next day, and the girls asked her if her boyfriend did it to her. She said she didn't have a boyfriend, but one of her classmates had seen her at the health department and demanded to know who he was. She said she couldn't tell them, and they didn't know him anyway. When they circled her, wanting to know, she said it was some older boy at the trailer park."

Beth listened attentively. As a social worker, she knew you learned more that way. She murmured appropriate sounds to let Missy know she was listening, realizing Missy needed to talk about these issues in her own life.

Missy's nostrils flared and her eyes flashed. "One of those stupid girls told her she was lucky to have an older boyfriend, and even said she'd always wanted to 'do it' with someone older and asked Candy if she thought he'd be willing to 'do her.' She said older guys were more experienced and could teach you a lot. Ugh!" Missy looked out the window. "'Course she couldn't tell them, so they assumed they were planning to get married when she turned eighteen. They thought it was cool: romantic. Candy begged them to keep her secret, and they said they would because it was statutory rape, and they guessed she didn't want him to get in trouble. She shoulda gone to someone." Beth agreed. "But she said her mom loved him, and she didn't want to break them up. Man, I would have."

"But you've learned to trust the adults in your world, Missy. Your mother and your pastor have always been there for you. You had somewhere to turn. Candy has me, and John, and now Martha and Joe."

"Martha's nice. So is Joe. I've always liked Joe."

Beth smiled. "Me, too, he's one of the good guys—and speaking of good guys, here comes mine." As they turned into the driveway behind Beth's house, the back door flung open and two little boys ran out into the yard, their father close behind them with their little girl in his arms. The boys got to the car before her husband did, but his face lit up when he saw her. Beth stepped into his embrace and lifted her face for his kiss.

The kids scampered around Missy, remembering her from when she lived at Hope House. "Back off, Kids, she's staying here," their father said. He put his arm around Missy and gave her a peck on the cheek. "Welcome—come on in. I got a pizza, Beth."

"We've had too much pizza lately, honey. I'm sorry."

"We won't have to make the boys eat tonight," he said. Beth's daughter was reaching for her, so she took the little one, dropping kisses on her neck until she giggled. After all the kids were fed, bathed, and down for the night, Missy sat with the couple in the family room. Beth snuggled up to her husband, and he put his arm around her, drawing her close.

Beth reached in a drawer underneath the couch. She handed Missy a book about marital relationships. "I'm going through this with Candy, and John is going through it with Joe."

Her husband flipped the cover. "My favorite book," he said with a grin.

"When your time comes, get this book. It's the best on the market," Beth told Missy.

"Is it Christian?" Missy asked.

Her host laughed. "Yes, it is," Tom said. "God's really comfortable about sex. He created it, you know."

"I don't have to worry about it for a long, long time. I have to finish college and get a job. Mom wants to get her RN degree." Missy stood. "I need to be excused—it was a long drive today, but I made it on time for the party."

"We'll go to Hope House tomorrow. John wants to talk to you about Jimmy." Beth embraced her. "'Night, Honey, sleep well."

Missy shuddered. "I hope I don't have nightmares, talking about all this stuff."

"Do you still have bad dreams?"

"Ever since I got back to the house where it happened. I hope I get a big enough scholarship to live in the dorm next year."

After the teenager left, Beth's husband asked "What did you talk about that upset her?"

"She remembered her rape experience, and she's worried about marriage. She sympathizes with Candy."

"Joe's the sweetest kid I know. He'll treat her well. It's good with the one you love, hmm?" Beth heard the love and the wanting in his voice, so she wasn't surprised when he added, "You wanna go try?'

"We don't have to try. We're experts at this."

"Always something new to try—I've been looking at that book."

"Don't get too fancy. You know I'm not as well coordinated as you are."

He chuckled. "This will all be on me, Baby."

Preparation for Love

At Hope House the next day, Beth stuck her head in John's office. "Is Joe coming in today?"

"He'll be here in about a half an hour."

"Missy told me last night Candy's abuser used to bite her breasts until they bled. I thought I'd pass that on. It's amazing she's nursing—but very healthy for her."

John jotted down a note. "Thanks, I'll tell him gentle on the breasts. Is Missy here?"

"She's in the kitchen with Ginny."

"Send her in. I have some suggestions for her brother."

"Will do, John, thanks."

Beth spent several hours in-taking another resident. When they finished the interview, she found Ginny alone in her upstairs office, paying bills. She sat on the comfortable sofa in her bedroom. "How's our housemother today? Gladys is a sweetie, but quite broken."

"I marvel at the resilience of the human spirit. These girls have been through awful stuff. How's Candy doing? They're leaving this weekend, right?" She fixed each of them a cup of tea and sat beside Beth.

"She hadn't read her homework, so I'm reading it to her. She squirms, but vows she loves Joe and wants to have a good marriage. Why don't we pray for her, and Gladys, too?" The women bowed their heads—prayer was the cornerstone of their work at the maternity home.

When Beth left, she went over to Candy's and found Missy there. "You found it!" she said after she pushed her way in. "Nice not to have to wait for double deadbolts to open."

"It's nice not to need double deadbolts," Martha said as she ushered her in the door. "Candy's getting Eddie down. "I'll run to the store for groceries and be out of your way. How's she doing, Beth? I know you can't say."

"She loves Joe. We'll keep praying."

"Maybe I shouldn't, but all I feel is joyful relief that two sources of evil have been removed from the streets."

"I understand, Martha. Ginny and I were talking today about the resilience of the human spirit. With God's help, we can do all things."

"Hi, Beth." Candy walked into the room, the infamous book in her hand.

Missy hugged her and said she'd better leave. "I told Cathy I'd come by today. I'll see you tomorrow."

After Beth and Candy went to the couch and sat, Beth pulled her Bible out of her briefcase. "I want to start here, in the Creation story." She quietly read and then stopped, pointing at a verse. "Can you read this?"

"And it was good," Candy read.

"He told Adam and Eve to be fruitful and multiply, and He made them sexual beings. That means the marriage relationship is good."

"You'll be proud of me. I read two chapters. And…I touched Joe…there." Beth waited. "I read about what it was like for men, and asked him how he felt. He asked if he could show me, and he put my hand on his…on his…you know." Beth named that part of the male body, and Candy bobbed her head. "It was really swollen. I asked if it hurt, and he said it did, and that's why he took lots of cold showers. He said sometimes he has to relieve himself, and he showed me that part in the book where it says if the wife is unable to, you know, do it, sometimes a man has to do it for himself. But he said he mostly got relief in dreams about me. He's really looking forward to this, Beth, and I want to make it good for him. He's waited all this time."

"That's my girl! John told me Joe prayed for the gift of celibacy, and he thought about Joseph, Mary's husband, who waited until after the birth of Jesus."

"I think I can do this. We're kissing a lot heavier now, and I've felt tingly."

"Feels good, doesn't it?"

Candy took a deep breath. "It does. I trust him. Thanks for making me do this—you know, study."

"I have a few more things for you," Beth said and pulled a bag of oils out of her purse. "You can give each other massages with this."

Candy picked up a tube. "The nurse at the health department gave me that."

"That is to show you what *not* to buy. These smell better and feel better."

"Do you use this?"

"Not always. My husband is a good lover, and we've been married a long time. By the time we're at that point, my body has made its own moisture. But you're young, and both inexperienced. This is good for honeymooners."

"Oh. Okay. Thanks." Candy said, turning the bottles over in her hand and reading the instructions.

"My pleasure—and yours, too." Beth's eyes twinkled. "You read these two chapters? Do you have any questions?"

Beth thought, for the millionth time, how she and Ginny were always telling girls things their mothers should have told them *What is wrong with us? Even in the church we don't prepare our kids for the culture in which we live. That's why even good girls get pregnant.*

"I don't know what I would have done without you, Beth," Candy said. "I love Martha, but she was abused in her marriage, so I don't talk to her about it. Missy was over this morning, and she said you'd talked to her. She said she didn't ever want to have sex, but I told her it was different when you love someone and want to make him happy. I do want to make Joe happy."

"I told her the same thing. But husbands aren't truly happy, Candy, if their wives don't enjoy making love."

"Really?"

"Yep, so be sure to express your pleasure. And tell him if you don't like something. He wants to please you."

"Joe said that—he wants to please me. He promised not to hurt me."

"He'd never hurt you intentionally, so if he makes a mistake or does anything you don't like, you tell him."

"I will. I think I can do this. I really do."

"You are a good, brave girl, and full of love. You'll do fine. Do you want to pray before I go?" They prayed, and Beth asked her if she needed her to come again before they left on Friday.

"I don't think so. I'll call if I have any questions. Mom goes back to work tomorrow, so I'll have time to read."

Martha took Candy to her appointment later that afternoon, and the doctor said it would be fine for them to go on their vacation.

The Honeymoon

The Renaissance Hotel gave the couple a week in their penthouse, and a limo took the three of them there on Friday afternoon. The luxurious car drove around to the back of the hotel, and the chauffeur opened the door for them, pointing to the service entrance. This arrangement threw off the press and the crowds wanting a look at the famous hero.

The limo driver set their bags inside and left. Immediately, staff gathered, picking up their suitcases and leading them to the elevator. Joe looked around at the grey concrete walls of the hotel's basement; they both appreciated the hotel's efforts to give them some privacy.

Joe cradled the sleeping baby, but still managed and to put a hand under Candy's elbow and guide her to the elevator.

The service microphone chirped in the bellman's lapel as he announced they were on their way, and they would not stop at the lobby floor. Candy watched the numbers light up—12, 13, 14, penthouse. She glanced at Joe, but he was looking at Eddie. Their guide stepped off the elevator and swiped the card in the door. Candy gasped. It was a palace!

"It's the nicest suite in the hotel, Ma'am." Several staff members were waiting. One was setting up the crib, and Joe showed him where they wanted it. Since they had several rooms, he put it in the other small bedroom

"Mrs. Long," a lovely Hispanic maid said, "I want to thank you for what you did. My daughter was killed by her boyfriend. It was very brave, what you did. Is your mother-in-law all right?"

"She twisted her knee when she dropped to the floor, but she got to the side so she didn't get shot. Thank God, she's fine."

The others pretended not to listen. One woman adjusted the beautiful arrangements of gladiolas, chrysanthemums, and other colorful flowers Candy didn't recognize, while another flipped out the crib sheets with a snap and tucked them neatly around the baby mattress. Two bellmen walked their bags into the bedroom and set them on the luggage racks. The older one showed them the mini-bar and told them to disregard the prices, because their entire stay was a gift.

"You may order room service for every meal and never leave the room, but if you want to go downstairs, call ahead and we'll seat you privately. If you want a sitter, we'll provide one. We have dancing tonight and tomorrow. Call if you want anything. We're proud you selected the Renaissance, and we want your stay to be perfect. Your ice is here, and the bar is stocked and on the house. Now, is there anything else?"

Joe reached into his pocket for a bill, but each staff person in the group shook his head. "Please," the maids and bellboys said, "We're honored."

When the door closed, Candy asked, "Is this is what I get for killing someone?"

Eddie lifted his head at the sound of his mother's voice and reached for her.

"This is some place," Joe exclaimed, wandering around from room to room. They had a huge living room with a big-screen TV, two desks, a sofa and several large comfortable chairs. In addition to the smaller bedroom, which was larger than theirs at the apartment, a master bedroom had a bed as big as their entire bedroom at home, a bathroom with a tub for two (he liked *that*), and another big-screen TV. He squatted in front of the bar, pulled out two Cokes and a bottle of water, and dropped some ice in the waiting glasses. Walking over to the chair where Candy sat nursing the baby, he gave a courtly bow and presented her with a Coke and the bottle of water.

"I can't believe this, Joe."

"Don't get used to it, Kiddo, I'll never be able to put you up in a place like this!"

"All I need is you."

Joe sat on the wide arm of her chair. "Aww, you say the sweetest things, Mrs. Long." Tucking a piece of her hair back behind one ear, he leaned in to kiss her neck. "You and Eddie are my world, Candy. Thank you for marrying me."

"Thank *me*? I can't believe you said that. You married a seven-months-pregnant female."

"She was still the most beautiful girl in the world. I looked up at you coming down those stairs, and I pinched myself. I couldn't believe I'd gotten so lucky. Missy really did it up special, didn't she? Flowers all the way down the stairs, on every side table, linens on the dining table. Everywhere I looked I saw beauty, but especially coming down the stairs toward me."

"I wanted to wait until I wasn't so fat, but you convinced me."

"I wanted Eddie to be mine and to have my name."

"I love you, Joe."

"And I love you. You weren't fat—I used to stare at your ankles in class. You have beautiful legs. I can't wait 'til summer, when you'll be wearing shorts."

She looked up at him and got lost in his eyes. Eddie grunted and rooted around. The nipple had slipped out of his mouth. She moved him to the other side.

"Does he hurt you when he nurses?"

"No. I can feel my belly tighten. Isn't that funny?"

"Didn't the doctor tell us those contractions made your womb go back to normal faster?"

"He did, and the pediatrician said he'd have fewer allergies and probably avoid braces."

"Good. I can't afford those either."

"You're going to do well. You're at the top of your class. You'll probably be rich, and won't want anything to do with a beautician."

"Don't count on it. You're stuck with me." Joe crossed over to the couch and picked up the remote. "You want to look for a movie? I wonder if those are free, too."

Candy pulled her shirt down and tried to get up from the deep, overstuffed chair with the baby. She floundered.

Joe moved to help her up. After giving her a hand, he took Eddie. She sat beside him, and they scrolled through the movies, selecting a light romantic comedy. It was cute, and they shared some laughs, playing with the baby between them on the sofa. He rolled from one side to the other to look at first one and then the other.

"He's gonna roll over before we know it," Joe observed. When the movie was over, he suggested he take the baby for a walk after she fed him. "You look tired. Why don't you take a nap? When I get back, we'll order room service."

No one recognized Joe and Eddie. Candy was the celebrity. He bundled him up and walked him down the street, window shopping, wishing he could buy everything in the stores for his wife and son. His chest puffed out as he saw his reflection in the window. He was not the skinny, scared kid he had been six years ago, when he'd tried to protect his mother from Scooter Long's rage. After the trial and his dad's imprisonment, he and his mother left Kentucky. His tongue found the cap on the tooth Scooter knocked out; his mom had to have her whole jaw rebuilt. At sixteen, he'd dropped out of school to work construction and dirty, heavy jobs, digging ditches, building sewer lines. Now he was tall, almost six feet, and muscular. He looked down at his fine son. He was married, a family man.

Candy was young. She'd turned eighteen in November, the month they married. She was older than her years, a survivor, who had left four years of hell behind her when she got pregnant and left the ratty trailer where she lived with her mother and her sleazy boyfriend. He would protect her. He prayed as he walked, hoping against hope that tonight they would experience all God intended for their marriage.

Eddie wasn't crying when they returned to the room, but he was making lots of happy noise. He peeked into the bedroom and saw Candy pushing her sleep-tousled hair off her face. She had taken off her clothes and put on the new robe. When she stretched, it gapped open, and he got a glimpse of her body. His own tightened at the sight. When he spoke, his voice cracked. He cleared his throat and started again.

"We're back; lots of fresh air made us hungry."

She patted the bed beside her, and he crossed the space quickly. "I'll feed him while you read me the menu." She pulled the top of her robe open to nurse, but held it closed below.

He gently brushed her hands away. "I like looking at you. Your body is beautiful. Do you mind?"

She shook her head, but blushed and kept her eyes down. He tucked his finger under her chin, leaned over the suckling babe, brought her face up, and kissed her deeply. He was gratified to see her smoky eyes darken and reluctantly got up to find the menu. They made their choices, and he placed the order.

Handing Eddie to him, Candy went into the bathroom, emerging in the grey silk pajamas Missy brought her.

Joe's eyes lingered over her. "That's nice."

"Missy and her mom bought these. I've never had silk pajamas before." She stood in front of him.

He set the baby on the bed and caressed her, running his hands across the smooth, soft material. He pulled her close, stroking her arms and her back. She shivered and he chuckled. "Like that, Mrs. Long?"

She leaned her head on his chest and nodded against him. Eddie rolled and kicked, and she said, "You're right. He may just roll over this week."

Joe dropped down on the bed, pulling her with him. "If all those party things are as nice as this, you're gonna kill me this week." He kissed her neck, moving up to behind her ear. "But I'll die happy." Hearing a knock at the door, he said, "Oops. Dinner's here."

Both of them tried to act casual when the waiter rolled in a table, covered with white linen. In the center stood a slender vase containing a red rose, and the waiter moved to a closet and brought out two chairs, padded with red velvet. After he set them down next to the table, he asked if they were ready. He seated Candy and lifted the lids from the plates, releasing a succulent aroma.

Candy could no longer pretend to be unimpressed. She leaned over and smelled the juicy steak. The waiter fussed around, grating pepper over their salads, pointing out the chocolate pie, and asked if they needed anything else. When Joe offered him a tip, he shook his head, saying this was for the lady.

When the door clicked shut behind him, Joe took her hand to say grace. He winked. "My wife, the hero!"

After the murmured amen, Candy took a bite and looked up in amazement. "I've never tasted anything like this. How can steak be so tender? And the flavor!"

"We can't afford beef like this," Joe said, "but I ordered medium. This looks raw to me."

"The menu said pink and warm in the center."

Joe poked with his fork. "Looks bloody and red to me—next time I'll order medium well, but it's good."

"The flavor is wonderful. I'm going to have to figure out how they do that."

"It's a prime cut—and we can't afford it. We'll stick to marinating the cheaper ones."

By the time they got to dessert, Eddie was getting restless in his seat. Joe jiggled him on his lap while Candy spoon-fed daddy his pie.

"Thanks. I never could have finished my dessert with him on my lap."

"He would've been demanding his own." Candy took him over to the chair and nursed him, and Joe watched her gentle hand soothing his dark hair off his forehead. "He doesn't have as much hair as he did when he was born," he said.

"He has lost a lot, hasn't he? But he's still a beautiful baby."

"Like his beautiful mommy—but we'll have to start calling him handsome soon. I'll entertain him while you soak in a tub. Would you like that?"

Joe pushed the cart into the hall and put the chairs in the closet. He looked out the window, watching the cars turn their headlights on as they moved through the streets below. "I never could have afforded to give you a honeymoon like this."

Candy saw from the stiffness of his back that it bothered him. Shifting the baby to her shoulder, she walked up behind him and leaned her head on his back.

Eddie's little baby fingers felt Joe's neck, and he turned around to gather them both into his arms.

"I've never had what you've given me, Joe. The apartment is really nice. I lived in a rusty beat-up trailer, where the wind came through the walls. Sometimes if I left my homework on the floor, the pages would flutter. Hope House is the only *house* I've ever lived in. You gave me a home. You gave my baby a father. I don't know why they're doing all this."

"I do. In a world where right is wrong and wrong is right, Columbus found a hero. You did right, and for once it was recognized. That reward money will pay for your beauty school, Candy. God really has blessed us."

"I still struggle, being blessed for killing a man."

"You need to get over that. He would have killed Mom, and probably you, too, and Eddie."

"He told me he was going to rape me, and kill you."

"He would have."

She shuddered. "When you got there, I was on the floor. Weren't you home early?"

"I felt like I had to be home. I blew off the review and caught the first bus. I saw it pulling off and ran after it, screaming. It was the longest, slowest ride ever. I was sure I had to be home, but I didn't get there soon enough."

"I was drifting, and you pulled me back. I heard your voice and fought my way back."

Eddie had managed to wiggle his way next to Joe and started to suck on him. Joe stepped out of Candy's embrace, chuckled, and pulled the little leech off his neck. "He must want the other side."

"He does. I'll take him." She went back to the chair and settled him on her other breast. She was quiet, but then said, "I thought I was going to die."

Joe lowered himself at the foot of the big chair and leaned against it. "I came so close to losing you." He shook his head, repeating "Thank you, Jesus," over and over. He looked up at her. "I would have taken care of Eddie, you know."

"I know. But I'm glad you didn't have to—I'm here now!"

"When we got to the hospital and they took you straight to surgery, I couldn't even pray. John came in and put his arms around me. I lost it then.

I told him I'd never made love to my wife. I don't know what the other people in the waiting room thought, but he told me I would, that people were praying, and that you were going to make it."

Hearing a burp, Joe looked up. "Ready for me to take him? You go soak."

"You're so nice to me, Joe."

"I'm your husband, Baby."

"I've known husbands like Lester and Scooter. You are one in a million. I can't believe you're mine."

Joe stood and pulled her to her feet. "Go. They have nice stuff in there for the water. Rest. We'll be fine."

"I took a nap."

"Good." Joe took her in with an intense look, his dark eyes smoldering. *Hopefully I'll keep you up tonight. God help me to do this right.* He patted her gently on the backside. "Go on."

Joe's Reward

He stared after her, fighting his growing need and trying to concentrate on Eddie. When she got to the bedroom door, she turned, giving him a shy smile, and her eyes were full of promise. She waved before she disappeared into the bathroom and closed the door. She had set the book and her robe on the counter already. She turned on the water, sprinkling some fragrant crystals under the stream, and climbed in the huge tub, clutching the book in her hand. She wanted to read a few things again.

The water slowly filled the big tub. *Maybe it would be nice to share this tub. Joe would like that. God, help me to be a good wife.*

When she emerged, she wrapped her robe around her and went looking for her men. She heard what sounded suspiciously like a giggle and Joe's deep voice. He was lying on the floor, playing airplane, waving Eddie in the air. A long string of drool broke off, hitting Joe in the face. He sat, laughing, and said, "Great shot, Boy. You got your daddy." He wiped his face.

Daddy, my baby has a daddy. I've never had a daddy. Candy choked on a sob.

Joe stood, alarmed, and crossed the room in long strides. "What is this? I sent you to pamper yourself and you come back in tears?"

"My baby has a daddy. You're the hero in this room, Joe." She put her arms around him. "And I love you."

Hoisting the baby higher on his shoulder, Joe put one arm around her and drew her close. She freed one hand from her husband's waist and curved it around Eddie's head as they kissed.

"Wait, I want to do this right," Joe said. He put the baby on the blanket on the floor and took his wife into his arms. He kissed her thoroughly, and felt pleased at her response. He wanted to bring her closer, but he worried about the strength of his need—no sense frightening her.

She pulled him closer. "It's all right, Joe, I know you want me. You've never kissed me like this before."

He groaned. "I didn't dare. I couldn't. I was waiting." This time he devoured her, and they broke apart, breathless when Eddie whimpered. "Good thing he's too little to tell tales."

"I want him to grow up knowing his parents love each other. I want him to be happy and secure. Kiss me again."

"Good plan," Joe said as he obeyed her command.

By the time they stepped back, Eddie was red-faced and crying. "He doesn't look too secure and happy right now, Mommy," Joe said as he scooped Eddie up to his broad chest and patted his back. "Sorry, Kid, Daddy needed a turn." The baby hiccoughed and drew quivering breaths.

Candy took him, walking to the big chair. "Now listen, Little Man, you're going to have to give your daddy some time with Mommy if you ever want to have brothers and sisters."

Joe grinned. "That sounds like a plan.

"Why don't you catch a shower while I get him down?"

Joe went into the bathroom and saw the marriage manual on the floor. He opened where she'd been reading. He read a few paragraphs and smiled. He practically had the thing memorized. He set the water and walked into the bedroom to gather his pajamas. After he showered, he dressed and went back to the living room, toweling his hair. They weren't there. Hearing a sound from the small bedroom, he found her shushing the baby. Her hand rested on his back until his legs stopped moving. She was leaning over the crib, and the soft robe gracefully cupped her bottom.

She straightened and tightened the belt. Seeing Joe, she whispered, "He's down."

Joe found words stuck somewhere down his throat, so he simply nodded.

"I'll be just a minute, okay?" Candy went into their bedroom, and he trailed behind, hoping his tongue wasn't hanging out. She wasn't in the bathroom long before reentering their room, wearing a white, lacy gown with pastel embroidery across the bodice.

Joe had seen her garishly made up, and watched her transformation from a rough, trailer park girl to a soft, lovely Christian woman. He'd even watched her grow large with child, but he's never seen her like this. She looked virginal.

"Beth and Ginny made this for me. Isn't it pretty?" She walked over to the bed and sat beside him where he was leaning against the headboard.

"It's pretty, but you are prettier." He tugged on her hand and drew her down. "Can I do this?" With her permission, he gently lowered her to the bed and stretched out beside her. He looked deeply into her eyes, and she didn't blink. He covered her mouth with his own, and her arms crept around his neck, drawing him closer.

In the bathroom, Candy had applied the gift from Beth, but she didn't need it as her body responded to his touch.

"I'm scared, too you know, Baby," Joe whispered.

"Why?"

"I got saved as a teenager, and made a promise to God to be pure for marriage. I've never done this. I want to be good for you."

"You will be, Joe. I know you will."

Joe held back, trying to slow himself down, and they did what lovers do.

Eddie slept well, thankfully, and didn't wake up until around two.

When Candy got up to tend to him, Joe stirred. "Are you okay?"

"I'm wonderful. Eddie's awake." The baby generally didn't wake much at night, and Candy moved quietly in the darkened room. The hotel staff had provided a rocking chair in the small bedroom, and it wasn't long before she had him back down.

Joe was coming out of the bathroom when Candy came into their room. She took care of her bathroom chores, returned to the big bed they shared, and slid into his arms.

"I hope you're you really 'wonderful.' I promise I'll get better at this. John says I'll get better with practice."

"That was pretty awesome, but if we get better, let's practice some more."

"A good wife, who can find?" Joe quoted.

"Was that good for you, Joe?"

"Oh yeah, it was good."

"Beth read to me from Genesis and reminded me God made us and it was good. I prayed to be good for you."

Joe tightened his arms around her. This time he was able to take more time, and it was even better.

Candy was sleeping soundly when Joe heard the baby again about five. He went into the small bedroom and changed him, but he couldn't do anything about Eddie's hunger. He shushed him and carried him into the master bedroom. He looked down at his waking wife, her light brown hair spilling over the pillow, and his heart swelled. Their first night together, their first real night of marriage, had gone better than he hoped.

Candy's eyes opened. "Did I sleep through his crying?" She pushed herself up. "I can't believe that! I'm such a bad mother."

"You are not. I heard him shuffling around and got him before he started to cry. You were sleeping so well I hated to wake you."

"I've never slept that well, ever, in all my life."

"Married life must agree with you, Mrs. Long." He settled the baby in her arms.

Candy blushed, looking at him covertly through half-closed eyes. "It does." She pulled at the ribbons at the top of her gown and reached for the baby. Since it didn't fall open and she was holding Eddie, Joe gently pulled it down to free her for nursing. She looked wondrous as the soft touch of his hand skimmed across her.

Remembering what John had told him, Joe had been careful last night, but seeing the softness in her eyes as she looked over the downy head, he thought they would try some more practicing later.

"Have you thought about what we should do today?"

"Practice?"

Joe laughed. "We do have the kid."

"Just kidding."

"I'm glad you're thinking like that."

"Thank God for Beth and John."

Joe stretched out beside her, crossing his long legs. "You've been through a lot these past few months."

"I've been through a lot the past five years. I never thought I'd ever be happy. I thought about killing myself, but once I got pregnant, I couldn't do that to the baby. Then Jesus came into my life and made me brand-new. You came into my life unexpected. Next to Christ, you're the best thing that ever happened to me."

"We're kind of confined here. I talked to the staff, and they said the media is hanging around like vultures, but they'd try to figure out how we could go downstairs. They have a nice gift shop. You want me to order breakfast?"

"Isn't it too early?"

Joe grabbed the remote from the bedside table and flipped on the TV. "Five forty-five. I think we can order at six." He crossed the room to pick up the room service menu. "Yeah, six. Whatcha wanna eat?" He sat on the edge of the bed, and they looked over the selections.

Eddie looked over his mother's breast at Joe and let the nipple slip from his mouth as he tried to curve his mouth into a smile.

"You're not done, Little Man," Candy said. She tugged on her gown to open up the other side and laughed as he grabbed hold and gulped greedily.

"He's his father's own boy—always ready to eat. He's getting fat!" Joe took the boy's pudgy legs in his hand and rubbed his fingers across his thigh. "Look at him."

"The pediatrician says he's perfect and gaining well."

"That's because he has a perfect mother. Are you hungry?"

"Starved!" Candy ordered a farmer's breakfast—meat, eggs, blueberry pancakes, and fruit; when it arrived, it was fit for a queen, served on thin china plates. The coffee pot was delicate, white with magnolias to match the china, but it plugged in to keep warm. Fresh maple syrup came in little disposable pitchers that she put into her suitcase later, for a memory. She also had English muffins and strawberry jam, and she ate every last bite.

They decided to attempt to go downstairs, so they made arrangements with the staff. The hotel manager, a Mr. Perkins, took them on the elevator to the second floor, asking if they could walk down one flight. When they pushed open the door, they saw a crowd in the lobby, keeping a close watch on the elevator. Mr. Perkins took her arm and pulled her down a side hall. Large yellow caution signs indicated a detour for painting. Looking up she saw a man on a ladder, but the kindly older man put his finger to his lips when she started to ask a question.

Mr. Perkins opened a door marked closed until ten and escorted them into the hotel shop. The smiling clerk in an elegant suit welcomed them and presented them with a $100 gift card.

"You have been so generous to us!" Candy exclaimed.

"Our pleasure," the saleslady responded.

Candy was self-conscious about her ratty blue jeans. Hope House had bought her maternity clothes, but she really didn't have much else to wear now, only her old clothes.

Joe leaned and whispered into her ear. "I have the money we saved for our honeymoon. Go ahead and pick out an outfit."

"Really?" she whispered, but when she looked at the tags, she pushed everything aside.

"Mrs. Long, perhaps you would like to look at our sale items," the clerk said. Catching their escort's eye, she added, "How much were we going to mark these down today, Mr. Perkins?"

The gentleman said, "I believe it was fifty percent—or was it seventy? When did we get these in?"

"Oh, it was months ago, Sir."

He waved his arm over a rack. "These will be seventy percent off, then, Mrs. Long. Take a look. Call me when you're ready to leave."

Candy picked out the softest pair of slacks she had ever seen and a matching blouse.

The saleslady suggested she pick out several more to take up to the room and try on.

She and Joe picked out gifts for Martha, Beth, and John—a nice apron for his mother, and trinkets for their counselors.

"May I?" The gracious lady reached for Eddie, and the amiable boy went right to her, grabbing her string of pearls.

"Oh, no, Eddie!" Candy extricated his hand from the necklace. "I'm sorry."

"I have grandchildren—he's a fine boy." She cooed over the baby and walked him over to some pinwheels, blowing them round and round and watching him stare.

Laden with packages and having maxed out their gift certificate, Joe and Candy were ready to go. Eddie went to his father with apparent relief, and the clerk said, "He knows his daddy, that's for sure. But he looks more like his mother. It's been a pleasure serving you, Mr. Long. The maid can return the items you don't want. I put the pinwheel in there for him."

"Thank you, Ma'am. You've been very kind."

After the brief call, Mr. Perkins, in his impeccable navy blue suit, reentered the store.

Candy suppressed a giggle as he gave a courtly bow. She thought maybe he'd click his heels, but he simply opened the door and waved them through.

"Let's go left," he said, indicating the way. He stopped at another door marked closed. "Would you like some refreshment?" He pushed open the door, and they followed him in to the empty tearoom where several ladies in frilly aprons were arranging mountains of delicate pastries on tiered plates.

Candy caught Joe's eye and patted her tummy.

"Perhaps we could make some selections for the room," Joe suggested. "We had a fairly large breakfast."

"Perfect," Mr. Perkins said, and he took a pastry box from underneath the counter. He stacked lemon cookies, almond pastries, and chocolate éclairs in the box and asked if they wanted anything else. They said no, but he added some tea sandwiches before taking them out the back door, assuring them he would have a fresh pot of coffee sent up.

When Eddie tuned up, Mr. Perkins apologized he'd kept them too long and led them to a service elevator. "This isn't the loveliest part of the hotel, but we are trying to protect your privacy. As you saw, quite a few media and plain gawkers are waiting to catch a glimpse of our hometown hero."

Candy tucked her hand in Joe's arm as the elevator mounted to the top floor. Joe's phone beeped, but they had no signal in the elevator.

"Thank you, Mr. Perkins, for everything. The hotel has been most generous," Candy said.

"The hotel is full, Mrs. Long. You create a full house. It's been a good gamble for us."

When he left, Candy said, "I can't believe it's 'Mrs. Long this and Mrs. Long that.' But I don't think I should ask them to call me Candy."

"They're pretty fancy here. I don't think any guests are called by their first name."

"I'm a hillbilly. If Missy hadn't been on me all the time like white on rice, I'd still be talking like a hick, with mixed up grammar, including double negatives."

"You learned fast, Candy. You're a smart girl, and now you're teaching me."

"You think I'm smart?"

"I know you are."

"I hope I'm smart enough to pass beauty school. I'll have to wait until June now."

"It's better. I'll be almost through with my classes. I'll get paid more as an apprentice electrician than I do at my night watchman job. Mom's looking for a night job, did she tell you?"

"Why?"

"She says she wants to get on at the hospital, and that's where the starting jobs are, but I think she wants us to have our nights alone."

"Was that her on the phone?"

"I forgot to check." Joe looked at the phone and called his mother back. "Really? That's incredible! I'll tell her. We can talk to the manager. Yes, Ma'am, we're having a great time! You should see this place. Yeah, that, too. Love you, Mom. I will." He looked over at her. "She sends her love, and I'm glad you're sitting down."

"What's incredible?"

"The Kentucky state troopers had posted rewards on Dad. He killed three policemen, you know." He paused. "It's fifty thousand dollars."

"Fifty thousand dollars! I've never seen that much money!"

"Apiece."

"What do you mean, 'apiece,' Joe?"

"Three men—fifty thousand for each policeman."

"Fifty thousand..."

"Fifty, one hundred, one hundred-fifty thousand."

Candy's mouth dropped open. "Are you kidding? You're kidding, aren't you?"

Joe went to answer a knock. Mr. Perkins himself carried in the fresh coffee. He pinked and turned away when he saw Candy feeding the baby. He set the coffeepot on the sideboard and retrieved a newspaper from under his arm. With his back to Candy, he said, "Thought you might like to read this, Mr. Long."

Joe scanned the headlines. "Local Heroine to Receive Reward." His eyes dropped down to scan the article. "Do they say how much?"

"No, but they want to present her the check this week. Do you want me to set up a conference room? I have a number for you to call."

Joe took the number written on a piece of paper and shoved it into his pocket. "My mother called. We'll be able to reimburse your expenses, Mr. Perkins."

"Stop, right there, Mr. Long. We've gotten a hundred thousand dollars' worth of marketing out of this. You don't owe us a dime. This suite would be sitting empty this week. If we have a news conference here, it will mean more business."

"Mr. Perkins, we're plain people, simple folks. We never could have afforded a place like this,"

"I know, Son, we've read all about you two. Those journalists have dug up lots of stuff." He lowered his voice. "Some of it unpleasant." With his back toward Candy, he whispered, "You might want to keep the newspapers and magazines away from her."

Candy overheard him and stood, tugging her shirt down. "Mr. Perkins, I know what I am. I'm poor white trash from a trailer park in Mississippi. I was raped by my mother's boyfriend from the time I was thirteen until I got pregnant at seventeen. Joe Long, an honorable man, married me when I was almost eight months pregnant so my baby would have a name. That's who I am, that's who I'll always be, so if you want us to leave, we will."

The hotel manager walked to where she stood in her ratty jeans and an Old Miss sweatshirt, swaying her baby. "You're wrong, Mrs. Long. You are brave and good. You are *not* trash—I doubt you ever were. You're a courageous woman of noble character who chose life for her child. Every one of our staff who has had the privilege of meeting you has been impressed. We are honored to have you here. Please, stay as our guests."

He touched her arm. "I'm a Christian, Mrs. Long, and I've had more opportunity to share the Savior in these few days than I've had in ten years. Only God can explain your story. I respect you as much as any person I've ever met." He turned to Joe. "And you as well, Sir. Let me know your decision." He handed Joe his card and eased himself out the door.

When the maid arrived later, she carried a large shopping bag. Giggling, she thrust it into Candy's hands. "In there's a white-blonde wig, dark glasses, and a long coat. We're trying to smuggle you out so you don't go stir crazy. If you've finished trying on those clothes, I'm supposed to take back the ones you don't want, but I'll be here a while."

Candy disappeared into the bedroom, and while Joe watched, holding the baby in the comfy chair, she tried on the outfits and chose two—the two Joe liked best. She carefully folded the rest and laid them in the bag. Between the gift certificate and their cash, she paid for everything they had chosen. After she had nursed Eddie to sleep and put him in the crib, she thanked the maid, handing her the returns, and told her she needed to rest and the bathroom was fine.

The maid left, and Candy hung the *do not disturb* sign on the door.

She glided across the room, dropped into Joe's lap and slipped her arms around his neck. She pulled his face down and whispered, in a sultry voice, "Wanna practice?"

Laughing, he said, "Oh, yeah. We might get good at this."

"If we practice enough," she said, leading the way to the big bed.

Officer Rod

While the newlyweds practiced, and Joe enjoyed the party gifts, Martha went back to work. The laundry wasn't open on Sunday, so she bustled around the house. She wanted to move Eddie's crib into her bedroom. The Christian radio station was playing so loudly that at first, she didn't hear the banging at the front door.

She cautiously asked who was there, and heard Officer Rodriguez's familiar voice. She left the chain hooked and peered out into the hallway. Seeing him, she quickly took it off and pulled the door open. "Why, Officer Rodriguez, what brings you here? I hardly recognized you without your uniform. Is everything all right? The kids are off on their delayed honeymoon."

"Yes, Ma'am. I thought I'd drop in to see if everything is all right."

"Oh, it's fine."

"You aren't frightened to be here by yourself?"

"Those we feared for years are both dead. Did you hear Candy's stepfather was killed in prison?"

"No, but I can't say as I'm sorry." Rodriguez made no move to leave.

"Me either." Martha stepped back. "I'm sorry. Would you like to come in?"

When he stepped into the living room, he saw the parts of the crib in the small hallway. "What are you trying to do?"

"We decided to move the baby into my room—he's getting bigger, and they won't have any privacy with him in their room."

"May I help you?" Rodriguez shrugged out of his jacket and crouched beside the scattered parts, picking them up and moving them into the bedroom with a single bed. "Where do you want this?"

Martha turned down the radio and pointed to the cleared space in the corner. "You don't have to do this, Officer. I know you're a busy man."

"I'm starting a week's vacation—call me Rod—this isn't a professional call. It's a...personal visit."

"Oh." Martha stuck out her hand. "Call me Martha."

Rod's strong brown hand took hers. "Marta. Do you have a screwdriver?"

"Of course—I took it apart in there." She hustled into the room Candy and Joe shared and returned with old tools.

"I'll be right back. I'll get mine out of my truck." He ran down the stairs and took them two at a time on the way up. With his power tools, Rod reassembled the crib in no time. He looked somewhat disappointed. "What else needs doing?"

She pointed to a box in the living room. "I bought a dresser for his clothes; I dreaded trying to put it together, but I hate to take up your time. Don't you need to get home to your family?"

"Marta, since my wife died, I go home to an empty house. All the children are gone. They have their own families." He crossed the room and opened the box, pulling out the pieces. He laid them out in an order, setting the bags of nuts and bolts beside them. Without looking at the directions, he began to fit the boards together, competently fastening them. "Here, could you hold this?" He handed her a drawer. "You could set it on your bed, if you like."

"I would have been all day doing this!" she exclaimed.

He chuckled. "Target, right?"

"Yes, how did you know?"

"I've put together about six of these, for my grandchildren's rooms."

"My goodness! How many children do you have?"

"Four boys and three girls: Carlos, Tomás, Jacinta, Ricardo, Linda, Juan, and the baby, Mérida."

"Seven?"

"Not all married, but with the esposos and kids, we have a crowd on holidays."

"I guess so."

"And you? Is Joe your only son?"

"I lost a few. Scooter didn't want any. I'm thankful to have Joe."

Rod frowned and looked up. "He didn't want sons? Joe is a fine man."

Martha sank down on the couch. "He is."

Rod noticed her hands shook as she swiped at her eyes. He shifted, reaching for the side pieces. "Do you know where you want this? We should finish it in the room, so we don't have move it." He carried the rest of the pieces into the bedroom and looked around. "Not much room against the wall because of the closet. Tomás' wife put hers at the end of the crib. The footboard made a wall, and she changed the babies' diapers on top of the dresser. She bought a piece of foam and covered it—worked out well."

"I can do that."

"She'll make one for you."

"I'm a seamstress, at the laundry. I make all my clothes, and I'm making some things for Candy now. She doesn't know it."

"You are a good mama, Marta."

"That poor child has never had a mother." Martha told him about Candy's mother, and his soft brown eyes glistened. "When she calls me Mom, it makes me so happy. Joe and I went through a lot with Scooter, but we always had one another. She had no one."

Sitting on the floor, Rod looked up. "How did you do it? How did you survive? In my work, I see this domestic violence all the time. I cannot understand. My parents were poor—farm laborers, illegals—but we were loved. Papá never hit us. Now Mamá, *she* would give us a swat." He laughed. "But never too hard. We knew we were loved."

"Lots of brothers and sisters?"

"Eight of us. We kids applied for student visas, and a degree in criminal justice gave me a good chance of getting citizenship. The police force needed Spanish-speaking cops. I got a job easily in L.A."

"How did you get to Ohio?" Martha asked.

"María, my esposa, didn't want our kids to grow up with all the Latinos on welfare. She made them speak English. 'If America gives us a new life in their country, we should speak their language.' And she would pop them upside the head if they didn't." He looked up. Martha sat on the edge of her bed, watching him. "We are proud people. We didn't want that—free lunches, free infant food." He shook his head vigorously. "No! I applied online and Ohio offered me a job. We came—only four bambinos then. María worked in a restaurant when I got off work. We did fine."

"All your children are citizens?"

"Yes—all born here. My boys do well. Carlos is a computer networker, and Tomás and Ricardo have a small engine shop. Jacinta is a teacher, and Linda's a nurse. Juan has a construction company, and Mérida is still in school."

"Amazing. You must be proud."

"My María, she made them work and study. They always have a job."

"She couldn't have done it alone. I wish my boy had had a father like you."

When he heard her voice crack, he looked up and saw tears trickle down her cheeks. He moved over and sat beside her on the bed, putting an arm awkwardly around her.

"Don't cry, Marta. You did fine. He is a good man, Joe. The man from the home—the counselor?"

"John Morgan, from Hope House," Martha supplied.

"He said Joe married Candy so the baby would have his name, and he waited to be a husband. That is hard for a man. I could see he loves her, and the baby." Rod looked away, adding quietly, "I have prayed for them because of what they have suffered. I hope they have a good week. It will be hard for her. Yes, Joe is a very good boy."

"I spoke to him briefly. He said they're having a good time."

Rod avoided her eyes as he went back and matched the side to the back of the dresser. "Now, I need to work. Enough talk."

When the dresser stood against the back of the crib, she had room to move around.

"How can I thank you? Now what will I do the rest of the week?"

"You can make a cover for a piece of foam," he said.

Martha looked at her watch. "It's five-thirty. May I fix you dinner? I have chicken in the crock pot."

Rod followed her into the kitchen. "I hate to be a bother."

"After all you did for me today! And I'd just be eating alone. Please stay." Martha reached under the counter for a rice pot.

"Arroz con pollo, my favorite. I cannot say no."

"Good." Martha measured the water and rice, and Rod helped her set the table. She measured coffee, and when he added an extra scoop, she said, "You like it strong."

His face curved into a smile, flashing white teeth. "Sí." Martha stood eye to eye with him, but he was stocky and broad—the kind of man who made you feel safe. His jet-black hair fell across his forehead, and she stifled a strong impulse to push it back.

When his eyes twinkled at her, she felt a lurch in her belly. *Goodness, what was that? I've never reacted to a man like that.* She turned the chicken, simmering in a tomato sauce. "I bet you like hot sauce. I don't know if I have any." She fussed around the spices. "Maybe if I add chili powder?"

Rod shook his head. He went to his tool chest, and tools clanked around. He returned with a small narrow bottle of hot sauce, holding it up to her. "I carry this with me."

"A dash of that and you can tolerate American cooking?"

Rod set it on the table and reached for the coffee pot.

Martha got two mugs out of the cupboard. At her first sip, she grimaced.

"Leche? Azucar? Milk and sugar?" Rod asked. He prepared both their mugs, and they went to the sofa in the living room to wait for the rice. Martha liked the coffee that Rod called café con leche.

When the timer went off, Martha served their dinner. She sat at the table and bowed her head.

Rod took her hand and blessed the food, but he held it a moment longer than necessary. "This smells wonderful," he said, shaking a generous dollop of hot sauce over the chicken and vegetables. He spooned more sauce over the rice and shook the small bottle a bit more. He offered her some. "Wanna try?" He sprinkled a drop on her rice.

She took a tiny bite and opened her eyes wide. "Oh!" she gasped, reaching for her coffee.

He watched, amused. "This is very good." She blinked, and he handed her a napkin to wipe her eyes. "Too much?" he teased.

She nodded, waving her hand in front of her mouth, but she laughed.

After dinner, he insisted he would help her clean up and seemed reluctant to leave. "Thank you for the food, and the company," Rod said. He picked his jacket up and shoved his hands in the sleeves.

"Thank you for all your help. What are you going to do on your week off? Are you taking a trip?"

"I'll stick around. I'm building a barbeque pit in my back yard."

"You are a talented guy," Martha said.

"Masonry is pretty easy—and Juan will help me." She walked him to the door, and he paused. "Could I take you to dinner after work tomorrow? To repay you for the meal?"

She protested it was entirely unnecessary, but by the time he left, he'd arranged to pick her up at the laundry after work.

Martha had worn nice clothes to work, and as closing time approached the next afternoon, she began picking lint off her pants. She was nervous. As a single mom, struggling to survive and keep a roof over her boy's head, she didn't date.

"I was locking up, but some big truck just pulled in. Go on. I'll wait," the lady at the front counter said.

"Probably my ride," Martha said.

"Got you a boyfriend, Girl?"

"No, he's the officer who saved Candy's life. He's taken it upon himself to look after me while the kids are gone."

Her friend peered through the blinds. "He's cute."

"He's nice," Martha said, pushing open the door.

Rod hopped out of his truck and came around to help her in. He took her to a small Mexican cantina, and she enjoyed the beef and bean fajitas that he ordered for her, speaking in rapid Spanish. He told her the proprietors were Mexicans who brought their help up from their home country, providing them with legitimate jobs. "We do that when we are lucky enough to make it. Like the Vietnamese and the nail shops. You are blessed to be American."

"We lived in rural Kentucky, and it was cold. Scooter was a coal miner. It wasn't too bad at first. He made good money, but he drank a lot. After he was crushed in a collapse and got disabled, he was always drunk—and he was a *mean* drunk. I worked at the hospital laundry. The bus dropped Joe off there after school, and we walked home together; I didn't want him home alone with his dad. He'd do his homework in the lobby, and everyone petted him. If only we didn't have to go home." Rod took her hand, playing with her fingers, but he sat quietly. "We lived in a shack, and the wind blew through the cracks in the wall. If I didn't get dinner fast enough, or he couldn't find the shirt he wanted, or..." Her head dropped.

"He beat you?"

She lifted her head proudly. "I kept Joey out of his way. I sent him to his room when Scooter was drunk, but one night when he was fifteen, he didn't go. He got between me and his dad, and Scooter took after him. I stepped between them. I remember hearing cursing and Joe shouting. The police came—the neighbors had called—and I woke up in the hospital several days later. The doctors said one more blow to the head would have killed me. The police questioned Joe and pressed charges against Scooter."

Rod brought her hand up to his lips and kissed her knuckles. He whispered, "*Jesucristo,*" but it wasn't swearing, he was praying for her.

She gave a shaky laugh. "Anyway, he was sent to prison. After school let out, we moved away. We knew he'd come after us when he got out, but they were supposed to call me when he was released."

"How did Joe turn out so good?"

"He joined a church when he was thirteen, and by the time he was fifteen, he was a leader. He says God gave him the strength to be with Candy and not touch her. He prayed to be like the other Joseph, the husband of Mary, and wait until after the baby was born."

Rod grunted. "I'm no saint, but maybe that qualifies him!"

"She was almost eight months pregnant when they married. Not too sexy."

Rod shook his head. "You women—you have no idea how sexy you look, ripe with child. My María..."

"Scooter didn't think I was attractive. That's how I lost my babies—he beat me in the stomach. And once, he kicked me down the stairs."

"I'm sorry, Marta."

"I've never told anyone all this."

"You have the most beautiful grey eyes," he said.

She blushed. "Where did that come from?"

"Like the mist in the valleys of Appalachia. You are lovely, Marta." She shook her head. "You are," he repeated, then asked, "Now, ice cream?"

She shivered. "Too cold."

He ordered again, and soon their waiter appeared with two coffees—prepared the way Rod liked them—and one large bowl of vanilla ice cream with hot dark chocolate steaming and streaming down the scoop, and two spoons. He dipped one spoon into the dessert and brought it to her lips. "You can't resist this."

One bite and she took the spoon from his hand. He chuckled, and they finished it together. They lingered over another cup of coffee, strong and hot, with lots of cream and sugar.

"I'm on vacation, but you work tomorrow. I'll take you home." Rod stood and held her coat, his hands lingering on her shoulders.

They pulled up in front of the apartment, and he came around the truck to open her door. He followed her up the stairs, noticing she was nervous. At the open door, he touched her cheek softly. "Good night, lovely Marta," he said. "I'll pick you up tomorrow."

"I can catch the bus, Rod."

"Ah, but then I would not see you." He touched her nose, his eyes sparkling at her, and turned to leave. "Be sure you lock up," he called back as he went down the stairs.

"Thank you for the wonderful dinner."

He flashed his amazing smile and waved.

Love Grows

After months of longing, Joe felt mellow and content, and he was pleased to see the tension seeping out of Candy. Her laughter was softer, her eyes didn't dart around, and she opened up to him like a flower in spring. They enjoyed the large tub together, and she lay quietly in his arms as his fingers traced her arms. She giggled and responded when his magical fingers caressed her tender places.

She whispered, "I love you, Joe," and he walked on the moon.

"We are blessed to have such a good baby," he whispered into her hair one night.

They didn't talk about the reward, which Candy couldn't believe was real, but the press conference was set for the last afternoon, right before their planned departure. When Joe pushed the baby stroller into the room Friday afternoon, the whispers began. He waited for Candy to enter through a side door. Kentucky state troopers on either side of her escorted her to the podium. Remembering her nervousness at the hospital, Joe watched her. She was confident, calm, and poised. Her eyes searched the room, lighting on him. His wife grinned and waved.

The press spun around, realizing the familiar father and baby had been in their midst all week. Flashes popped, and Eddie cried. Joe picked him up and put him on his shoulder. When he calmed down, the officers began their tribute and presented Candy with the check.

Taking a deep breath, she stepped up to the microphones to thank them. "I know many of you think I'm a bad person. I had a handgun, and I used it to kill a man. He was my husband's father, but he'd beaten Joe's mother all their married life. After the last beating, he was incarcerated because he almost killed her. He escaped and came to finish the job. He told me he'd kill her, and after he'd done that, he was going to rape me. I figured he'd kill me, too. My helpless baby was in his bed in the next room. My husband had bought me a gun and taught me how to use it because—as you have so graphically reported in these trashy articles—my mother's boyfriend had abused me throughout my teen years, and he wanted to come after me." Candy threw the tabloids on the table and lifted her chin.

"I prayed—can you believe that? I asked God to help me protect my mother-in-law and my baby. The gun was behind the cereal boxes, and I managed to slip it in my pants pocket. I heard Martha at the door and distracted him so I could call to her to get down. He shot the door over and over, and then he pointed the gun at me. I shot him. I'm not proud I killed a man, but I'm glad he's dead. I'm glad Martha is alive, and he'll never hit her again. May God forgive me."

One of the officers slipped his hand around her waist, while the other stepped up to the microphone. "We'll take no questions," the second policemen said, as the first officer led her to Joe.

Mr. Perkins appeared and took the baby while Joe gathered his trembling wife into his arms, flashbulbs popping all around them. She leaned against him, and he practically carried her as Perkins led the way through a back door. Hotel staff kept the other doors shut. He led them through the now-familiar bowels of the building to a waiting taxi. The driver opened the door, and Joe pressed Candy's head down as she crawled inside. Once she was sitting, he turned to take the baby.

"I don't know how to thank you and the staff here," Joe said, shaking Perkins's hand.

"Our privilege, Mr. Long. We hope you come back soon. Take care of her."

The minute Joe got in the back seat, Eddie lunged for his mother. Candy had tears streaming down her face, but she sniffed, holding out her arms. Joe put his arms around the two of them.

The taxi slowly moved off. "They told me to get out of here while they stalled. Where to? Just some advice, they know where you live. Anywhere else you can go?"

Joe reached for his phone and dialed his mother. She said she'd call him right back, and soon she did, giving him a location near a park.

"Officer Rodriguez will meet you there. He has a white pickup."

Sure enough, he met them. Joe handed up the car seat and while Rod fastened it in the back seat, Joe loaded the suitcases. He tried to pay the cabbie, who waved him off and wished them luck.

"This is a mess, Officer. You are kind to come get us. I don't know where to go."

"No problem. You're coming to my house." He looked in the rearview mirror at Candy, who was buckling herself in. "You okay, Candy?"

"We can't do that." Joe protested.

Rod looked across the seat and grinned. "While you and your wife were getting to know each other, in the Biblical sense, Marta and I have seen a lot of each other. Since you are the man of the household, may I have permission to date your mother?"

"I thought you had a family."

"My wife died ten years ago. My kids are grown and gone. We had seven of them, so we have plenty of room for you and your mother until this madness settles." Rod moved his truck into the traffic. "You can close your mouth, Joe." Joe did. "Your mother is an amazing woman. I like her—a lot."

"I don't know what to say."

"Say yes. We are of legal age, and probably wouldn't take no for an answer. But we—I'd—like your blessing."

"She's been through a lot, Officer..."

"Call me Rod. I know. She's told me about it."

"She doesn't talk about it. You don't know the half. She's a survivor."

"I know he killed her babies by beating her in the stomach and pushing her down the stairs. I know she protected you, worked in the hospital laundry, and walked home with you every day. When your father put her in the hospital that last time, she had to have plastic surgery. Her jaw was wired, and the entire dental school looked at her mouth. She grieved because you were in foster care. She's more than a survivor. She's overcome all that and kept her faith in God. I never thought I'd love another woman. I was married for twenty-two years when María died; we married when we were eighteen. She was much too young to die. I haven't dated, haven't looked, and haven't wanted another woman. But I think I love your mother—I haven't told her that yet, though. She's not ready to hear it."

"You are a fast mover, Off—Rod." Joe shook his head and looked back at Candy. "What do you think, Honey?"

"I think it's fabulous!" Candy said.

Joe shook his head. "Me, too—but if you hurt her, I'll make you regret it."

Rod laughed. "Scare me, why doncha? I hear you folks believe in the Second Amendment."

Laughter filled the truck. Joe reached across the seat and Candy took his hand.

"What have you and Mom been doing?" Candy asked.

"Sunday night, we put Eddie's crib in her bedroom and put the chest together. She fixed me a nice meal. Your mom sewed a cute cover for a piece of foam to go on top of the chest, to make a changing table for you. Monday night, we went to a Mexican cantina. Tuesday night, we watched a movie on TV at your place. She made meat loaf. Wednesday I fixed dinner for her at my place. Last night, we went to a movie at the mall. And tonight, my family is hosting a dinner. No one can believe I'm seeing someone. My daughter, Linda, met her Wednesday night when she popped over. Are you up for it?"

Joe took a deep breath. "Seems like it's a done deal."

"My kids want to check her out in the worst way."

"How many kids do you have, Rod?" Candy asked.

"Seven. They'll all be there, with their families. The last three aren't married yet, but Linda will probably bring her fiancé."

"How are we going to feed all these people?" Joe asked. "Mom works all day, I'm not asking her to feed that many people!"

"Carlos is the millionaire. He's having it catered."

"What does he do?" Joe asked.

"He's a computer genius—invents software, designs apps, that kind of thing. He and his wife rake in the dough. She builds networks."

"And the others?"

"Tomás and Ricardo have a machine shop. Jacinta is a teacher. Linda is a nurse, and dates a doctor. Juan is in construction, and my baby girl, Mérida, is still in school, studying graphic design this semester."

"You have successful children."

"They had a wonderful mother."

Candy leaned forward. "How old are they?"

Rod rattled off their ages, "Carlos, thirty-one; the twins, Tomás and Ricardo, twenty-nine; Juan, twenty-seven; Jacinta is twenty-five, Linda, twenty-three, and Mérida is nineteen."

"If your wife died ten years ago, Jacinta was fifteen, Linda was thirteen, and Mérida was only nine. How did you do that, being a cop?" Joe asked.

"My mamá moved in. We are a good family. Papá died about twelve years ago."

"Where does she live now?"

"Mamá lives with Carlos. She thinks she's raising his kids. They have a nanny, but Mamá watches her close."

"Will she be there, too?"

"Yes—she is what you call the matriarch."

"I'm terrified," Candy said. "I've never heard of such a big family."

"They are terrified. You are the hero with a gun."

"I hate that, you know," Candy said.

"I know. But you did well today. I listened on TV. It was a fine speech."

"I called my friend, Missy, in West Virginia. She helped me write it, and coached me over the phone. Was it okay?"

"Excellent. If I wasn't a man, I'd have cried—especially knowing Marta's story. She tells me your step-father was killed in prison, Candy."

"That's what I've been told."

Rod stopped his truck in front of a large Victorian house. It was old, but well-maintained, and reminded Candy of Hope House.

Eddie had fallen asleep in the car seat, and Joe tried to lift him out without disturbing him, but the baby rubbed his eyes and cried.

Candy lifted him to her shoulder.

The men carried in the suitcases, and Rod led them up to a large bedroom with a rocking chair, where Candy immediately sat down. Because they didn't have a crib, Joe put a blanket on the floor. The men tiptoed out, hoping the baby would finish his nap. Not long after, however, they heard him crying as Candy came downstairs.

The baby reached for Joe, hiccoughing soft little cries. Joe rubbed circles on his back, whispering. They decided he'd had too many changes, so his daddy settled him in the crook of his arm.

They chatted while Eddie dozed off, until Rod jumped up. "Oh, it's time to get your mother." He grabbed his keys and left on the run.

Hearing the door open, Candy stood.

"Hi, I'm Mérida. Linda's right behind me. We thought we'd set up the tables before the food arrives. You're Candy and Joe? Oh, look how cute!" A petite Latina leaned over the chair. "Come see, Lin."

Linda, a bit taller, but still not over 5'3", peeked at the baby and smiled. She wore scrubs, and her dark hair was caught up in a ponytail. "He's precious! I'll be right down, Mer. I'm going to change." Linda bounded upstairs.

Candy walked over to the kitchen. "May I help?"

Mérida had opened the silverware drawer. "Let's see, everyone is coming. That will be five, three, five, two, and Linda, Juan, and me. Plus you guys—Papá, your mother, and you and Joe. How many is that?"

Candy stared blankly. "I lost count."

"Carlos and Conchesca have three children. They are bringing a pack and play over here for the baby. That's five." Candy held up one hand, and Mérida laughed. "You'll run out of fingers." She pulled open a drawer and gave Candy a notepad and pencil. She wrote *5*. "Tomás and his wife have two." Candy added *4*. "Jacinta isn't married." Candy wrote a *1*. "Ricardo and his wife have one, and she's pregnant." Candy wrote *3*. "Then add me, Linda, and Juan." Another *3* went down on the paper. "You and Joe, your mother and Papá—I can't believe Papá has a girlfriend."

Candy added it up. "Twenty. We're feeding twenty people?"

"Welcome to the Rodriguez family—oh, add one more for Abuela. My grandmother will be here, too. She's fussed since she heard yesterday. How many brothers and sisters do you have?" Mérida could hardly believe both

Joe and Candy were only children. She stared at them. "I don't believe I've met an only child before."

"Who's an only child?" Linda asked as she came in, tugging her tee shirt over her jeans. She peered over Mérida's shoulder at the list. "Jacinta isn't coming."

"She's not coming to meet Martha and Joe and Candy?" She was astonished. "Why not?"

"She has a date with the creep."

"The creep?"

"Carlos doesn't like him." Linda explained. "He picked Jacinta up at the office, but he just sat in the car, honking."

"Oh, boy. I can hear Carlos. But it's the American way."

"It's rude, and it's not our way. Carlos went out to the car and made him come in. Conchesca said Carlos told him he was the oldest brother, and no one picked up his sister like that." Linda turned to Joe and Candy. "Who is the only child?"

"Both of them," Mérida answered.

Linda's dark eyes were sympathetic. "Must have been lonely, huh?"

Candy and Joe looked at each other. They both shrugged.

"It's what we knew," Joe said.

Tomás and Ricardo pushed open the door, carrying boxes. "You girls need help setting up?" Tomás picked up Mérida and tossed her. Like their dad, the twins were not tall, but square and strong.

Ricardo grabbed Linda by the waist, hauling her into a fierce hug.

She swatted him on the head. "Let me go, you big lug. Your breath stinks—what did you have for lunch?"

The brothers laughed, then noticed their company and sobered. "I thought Papá's girlfriend was coming later. I'm sorry. This is my brother, Tomás, and I am the handsome, dashing, and attached Ricardo." He laughed, punching his identical twin.

Joe stood to shake hands. "Joe Long—my wife, Candy."

"Oh, the—"

"Please don't say it," Candy interrupted.

The four siblings with identical pairs of black eyes regarded her. "I get it," Linda said. "Tired of all the hoopla, aren't you?"

Candy started to cry, and Linda took her in her arms. "I killed a man," Candy said. "Some call me a murderer, and some call me a hero. I'm neither."

"Go ahead and cry, Honey. We'll put this family in the call-you-a-hero category, all of us but Jacinta. She's hung up on guns. But it had to have been horrible. How scary! Papá was crazy until you pulled through the surgery."

"He saved my life—he and his partner."

"Papá would say it's all in a day's work, Candy," Tomás said. He patted her shoulder. "Let's get going. Carlos and Conchesca will be here soon with rest of the food. Where's Papá?"

"He went to get my mother at work," Joe said.

The brothers exchanged a glance and headed for the closet. They pulled out long folding tables and set them up in the large open space. "Juan took out some walls—you see the beams?" Ricardo pointed up. "They hold the ceiling. He put them up when he took down support walls. He's a smart kid, even if he is the baby."

"*I* am the baby, and don't you forget it."

"As if we ever could, Mer," Tomás teased. "Here's Papá now."

Rod and Martha entered and Candy's eyes popped open at the loud embraces, hugs, and greetings. So much laughter.

Joe watched his mother, as overwhelmed as Candy, but Rod had his arm securely around her waist.

"HOLD IT! Pipe down, everyone. This is the lovely Marta. Put on your best manners and introduce yourselves."

"Yes, Papá," the girls chorused. "I'm Linda—you met me Wednesday night." Martha remembered. "And this is the baby, Mérida—right, Mérida, 'The Baby?'"

Mérida bumped her sister with her hip.

Tomás stepped forward and took Martha's hand in his. "I am Tomás, and this is Ricardo. We own the machine shop. Juan will be here soon."

"Where are my son and daughter-in-law?"

Candy waved from the big chair. "Here, Mom."

"Hi, Mom," Joe said, with a twinkle in his eye. He held out his arms, and she hugged him, hard. Eddie reached for her, and she took him. The baby leaned against her with a sigh. "He missed you, Gram."

"I missed him," she said, kissing his cheeks.

Candy stood to give and receive her Martha hug. The house continued to fill up with Carlos and his family, Ricardo's wife and child, and Juan, the youngest brother. But the most commanding presence of all was the tiny abuela, the grandmother, who looked at Martha with snapping, steely eyes of coal.

"Come, tell me about yourself." She tugged Martha away.

"Mamá, por favor."

"If you like her Mario, I will, too, no?"

"It's too much, all of us at once," Rod protested.

"Hush. You are just the policía. But *I* am the abuela."

Carlos laughed, hugging his tiny grandmother. "And we all know who is the boss! May we eat, Abuela?"

"Sí. All the food. Come, eat."

Linda sat by the Longs, putting Martha beside her father. Once all the scraping of chairs was settled, silence fell, heads bowed, and Rod prayed. After he said, "Amen," clatter and chatter resumed, with much scrambling for favorite foods. Mamás filled their children's plates, and platters were passed around.

"This is enough food for an army," Candy whispered to Joe.

"This *is* an army!" he replied, juggling Eddie on his lap. Eddie held Joe's shirt in a tight fist.

After dinner, the two grandmothers drew apart to talk. Señora Rodriguez spoke with a heavy accent, and Martha had an Appalachian drawl, but the ladies got along well.

As Carlos took his grandmother's arm to help her down the front stairs, Rod took the other and said, "I told you you'd like her, Mamá."

"Sí, Mario, you were right. She is a good woman. I approve—but she is sleeping in your house?"

"In another room, Mamá, until the media leaves them alone."

"You will marry her."

"Shh, Mamá, she is not ready."

"She needs this family."

"I need her."

"It's time, my boy. You have been alone too long."

Joe watched Rod helping his mother out of the house, and when he leaned to kiss her leathery brown cheek, he also brought her calloused hands to his lips, remembering when she bent over strawberries picking in the fields, day after day. He said, "Te quiero, Mamá."

"What does that mean?" he whispered to Juan.

"He told his mamá he loves her. And he does. We all love her."

And Joe knew Rod Rodriguez was a good man, who would be good for his mother. He definitely approved.

Blinking rapidly, the old lady patted her son, leaning on Carlos heavily as she went down the stairs.

Embraced by a Family

After getting the Long family settled, Rod called Jacinta. He called until midnight, finally reaching her at 12:30.

"Papá, why are you calling so late? Is something wrong?"

"Yes, very wrong when the family has a fiesta to introduce the Long family and you are not here to meet them. Where were you? Who is this date who doesn't meet the family?"

"He's met Carlos. They had words. He's not into family."

"We are your family, Jacinta. If he is 'not into your family,' as you say, I have no respect for him. Carlos is a good judge of character. You should listen to him."

"You fuss all the time that I should be married, and I have a date and you still fuss."

"You are a teacher, this is late to be out."

"You are the policía. It is late for *you* to be up. It's Friday night, remember? I'm not a teenager!"

"I'm still on vacation. Juan, Joe and I will be finishing the barbeque pit tomorrow."

"Who is Joe?"

"He is Marta's son. Come tomorrow and meet my guests."

"Your guests?"

"The Longs are staying here until the media finds another story, another one to harass."

"I'll see. Maybe I can get by before Jeffery comes."

"This man you date is Jeffery? Let's hope his last name isn't Dahmer."

"Papá!"

"I kid, Jacinta. I only wish for Marta to meet mi preciosa hija. Por favor. *Please.*"

"You like this Martha, don't you, Papá?"

"Sí."

"Okay, I'll come give you my approval. I'm sorry I missed the fiesta, Papá."

Rod was pleased that Martha was off Saturday, a special day off in honor of Candy and Joe's return. Juan came over to help his dad, and Joe went outside with them. Martha visited with Candy. They tried on the skirts and blouses she had made, and Martha gathered up and loosened seams, talking with pins in her mouth.

"You and Rod are quite the item, Mom."

"He was only looking after me while you were gone." Martha shrugged.

"That's not the way I see it."

"It's the way I see it. I don't want the complication of a man in my life."

"Why? He's nice, and stable...and the way he looks at you!"

"Stop that. Stand still before I poke you."

"Yes, Ma'am."

"When you think we can go home?" Martha asked as she stepped back, tugging a sleeve.

"I don't know. I hate this! Everyone following us, shouting questions, taking pictures."

"You and Joe had fun?"

"We did. He was good to me. It was incredible. The hotel was so nice to us. They gave us food, a hundred-dollar gift certificate, free movies...I felt like a princess. The two of us had fun. Joe was wonderful to me. I enjoy married life." Candy blushed.

Martha pulled her daughter-in-law into an embrace. "I'm happy for you."

"I want you to be happy, too, Mom."

"I am happy. I'm proud of you and Joe. I'm sorry the surgery put off your schooling, but you'll have a good long time to nurse the baby and get strong. How do you feel?"

"I need to sit if I'm on my feet too long, but I'm good."

Joe pushed open the back door. "We're ready for lunch. Juan is here, and Jacinta is coming by."

The ladies had prepared sandwiches and drinks, but Jacinta ate quickly, because she was meeting someone. Rod was disappointed she didn't stay longer, but he was proud of his beautiful daughter, the teacher.

Rod saw Joe and Candy exchange playful touches and laughing responses. They'd come a long way.

But that night, Candy's scream pierced the quiet, bringing Martha and Rod into the hall in their night clothes.

"Shh, Honey, it's me. Shh," Joe whispered.

Eddie started to wail, and Candy said, "Give him to me." Then she said, "Oh, Joe, did I hurt you? Let me see."

"It's okay. It's okay." The conversation was muted into tender murmurs and whispers.

Loving an Abused Woman

"They're fine," Rod said. "I'm going back to bed."

"Joe took care of it," Martha replied. Looking down at her cotton gown, she folded her arms across her chest.

Rod carefully looked away, but he had noticed, and he tossed and turned before he slept, remembering how nice it was to have a warm body beside him at night. His bed seemed cold and empty. This woman was different from Maria. She was taller and thin, where his wife had been small and round. She was shy and quiet, and Maria was talkative, bubbly, and laughing—unless she was fussing. Martha never fussed, and if he coaxed a smile, he felt it was a great accomplishment. But when she smiled, the sun came out from behind the clouds, and she never expressed displeasure or lost her calm, even demeanor. It would take work—like Joe with Candy—but somehow, he felt it would be worth it. And, God knows, she deserved to be loved.

When Joe came into the kitchen Sunday morning, Rod took one look at him and asked what happened.

Martha gasped, and her son gave her a half-smile.

"Another lesson in loving an abused woman: never snuggle unless she has her eyes open. I terrified her. It was my fault. She won't come down because she thinks you'll hate her, Mom."

Martha pushed her chair back and went quickly to the stairs while Rod handed Joe a cup of coffee.

"Nothing to do for it anyway, the swelling will be down by tomorrow, but the purple will take a while."

"I've got to go back to school tomorrow. I remember Mom going to work, telling everyone she walked into a door. I understand—I'm sure not telling anyone my wife clocked me!"

Rod put his arm around Joe's shoulder. "I get that. Pretty little thing like that can shoot *and* packs a wallop."

Hearing the women come down the stairs, Joe prepared Candy's coffee and handed it to her, exchanging it for the baby, who reached for him out of Martha's arms.

"I'm sorry, guys. I know you heard me. It was awful. I can't believe I did that." She looked at Joe, set her coffee down, sank into a chair, and cried.

Joe knelt beside her, balancing as best he could with Eddie bouncing in his arms. "It's okay, Baby. I told them it was my fault." He glanced up. "She was having a bad dream."

Martha patted her back. "That I can understand, Candy." She handed her a wad of tissues. "Bad dreams come from the past, Sweetie, but they ease in time."

Rod poured himself another cup of coffee. "Wasn't your abuser killed in prison, Candy? Didn't that ease your fears?"

Candy blew her nose on a napkin. "I was told he was, but I can't wrap my mind around it. I keep dreaming he escaped like Scooter and he's coming after me. I can't do that again."

"I can certainly get verification for you, Honey," Rod said.

She looked up, and he stretched his arms out to her. She came to him, falling in his arms and resting her tear-stained face on his chest. He held her like an injured bird. He patted her back until she relaxed.

"What happened to your natural father?" he asked.

"He was a logger. Right after I was born, he was killed in an accident—a stack of logs rolled over and crushed him. I never knew him. I heard my mama didn't start drinking until after that, but I don't remember her sober. She would sleep with anyone who would supply her with whiskey."

"You've never known a real father," Rod said.

"Mama took up with Lester when I was about nine, and I was scared—something about the way he looked at me—and when I was thirteen…"

"You don't have to say any more. I'll get on this right away. Give me his full name."

She told him Lester's name, and that he was incarcerated at Parchman. He raised his eyes at that—the prison was notorious for housing Mississippi's most violent criminals. Obviously, Candy wasn't this perp's only victim. Excusing himself, he went into his office and made some phone calls. Soon the fax whirred, and he returned with papers in his hand. Signaling to Joe with a nod of his head, he indicated he should give the baby to Martha.

"I don't know how much of this you want to see, Candy, but I have the official autopsy report—knife wound to an artery—and some morgue photos."

Candy looked up at Joe and took his hand. "I'd feel better if I saw the picture and made sure it was him." Joe stood behind her while she looked, shuddered and said, "Yeah, it's him. He's dead. Thank God."

Rod heard Mérida come in the back door. She quickly felt the solemnity and looked at her father, who stretched out an arm for her to duck under.

"Candy needed some closure," he explained. "She's having nightmares about her abuser, so I pulled some strings and got her photos."

"He's really dead, Mer," Candy said. "The only thing left is to go see my mother."

"Oh, Sweetie, you can't do that alone, and I've missed so much work I can't miss any more," Martha said.

"Me, too, Honey. I may have to repeat this section," Joe added.

Mérida said, "I have mid-term break—two days before a weekend, next week. I can go with her."

Rod squeezed his daughter's shoulder.

"I hate to ask you to go to all that trouble. But she doesn't have much time. She's in a nursing home."

"Hey, Girl, it's what families do. We could make it fun—after the sucky part. You sure? You don't owe her anything after what she did to you."

"She needs forgiveness, and she needs Jesus. I've got to try."

"Okay, let's go MapQuest the trip. Can I use your computer, Papá?" He waved his hand. Mérida and Candy went into Rod's office. Candy said she'd nurse Eddie while they printed the information.

After they left, Rod said, "We need something besides coffee."

"I'll fix eggs." Martha pulled eggs and bacon out of the refrigerator while Rod set out frying pans.

"Sir?" Joe said. Rod raised his eyebrows in response to the young man's questioning tone. "Could I have a word with you?"

Martha looked between the two men. "I can get this."

Joe closed the door to the office, amazed to hear the two girls giggling, and sat beside Rod on the couch. "Thank you for what you did for Candy. I was almost jealous—I've been the only one for her, besides the Hope House counselors, but when you said she'd never had a father, I realized I never had one either, and I need some advice."

Rod leaned forward and gave Joe his full attention.

Joe continued, "Last night before we went to sleep, we had a disagreement. She wants to use the reward money to buy a house, and I said we needed to save it for emergencies, and put it away for Eddie's college. We're in no position to buy a house. Things happen: roofs need repair, a hot water heater goes out—we don't have time or money to handle that kind of stuff. She got all pouty and said she'd do with her money what she wanted." He dropped his eyes.

"I didn't say the right thing. I told her she could buy a house, but I didn't have to live in it. I shouldn't have said that." He looked at Rod, searching his face, and he blinked rapidly. "She rolled over and cried. No wonder she had a nightmare. I rejected her. John told me she was super-sensitive. She's only eighteen, you know."

"I didn't—those grey eyes look old as the hills—haunted eyes do that. How old are you, Joe?"

"Twenty-four. I've been taking care of Mom and me since I was sixteen. I dropped out of school and worked, but when Mom got a decent job, I decided to go to trade school. I had to get a GED. That's where I met her, in GED classes."

"I understand your position—hold on, let me text Mérida." Rod sent his daughter a text, asking her to divert Candy a while, and returned to the conversation. "You're right. A house is a big responsibility. She wants a nest for her boy, and the home she's never had, but waiting is better. She doesn't have a handle on financial things yet. Perhaps you should take this to your counselor."

"Maybe you could talk to us. She respects you. She loves you. You saved her life."

"All in a day's work, Son, but the two of you are special to me."

After breakfast Rod left Martha and Mérida to clean up while he talked to the young couple, gently correcting each one of them, and giving some financial advice. They agreed to use the small reward as planned, for Candy's schooling, and to put the rest away for the future. Rod talked to Candy about the expense of a home: taxes, insurance, maintenance, and the time it took to care for those details. With both of them in school, it made more sense to rent.

Then day lightened up. They didn't go to church because of Joe's face. After their late brunch, Joe and Rod snacked around the college play-offs while the ladies visited.

The front door banged open—Martha couldn't quite absorb the open-door policy of this family, but Rod was unperturbed.

His granddaughter—about four years old—ran across the room and threw herself into his lap. "Abuelo, you didn't come to church. Where were you? I'm going to be an angel in the Easter play, but I need a costume. Mrs. Francis gave me the material, but Mamá said she doesn't have time to sew a costume, and Bisabuela said her fingers are too knotted. What makes her fingers knotted, Abuelo?"

Martha chuckled as Rod sorted out his grandchild's questions. "I am a seamstress," she said. "I can do an angel costume." He looked over the child's dark, curly head and gave her a warm smile of appreciation. She would need her sewing machine and basket of supplies. They called the landlord to see what the situation was at the apartment. He told them journalists and gawkers still lingered—and their check was due.

The Apartment

Carlos went with Joe to the apartment building. As they approached, Carlos pointed to a sign over the door: *Home of Columbus' Hometown Hero*.

"If he's objecting to the crowds, he ought not to invite them, wouldn't you say?" Carlos said.

Joe approached the building, and several newspaper reporters recognized him.

"Where is your wife?"

"Where are you staying?"

"When will she answer questions?"

Carlos pushed through the group, making a path for him. They pushed through the door. After stopping at the landlord's apartment to drop off the rent check, they went upstairs to fetch the sewing equipment. Joe gathered up a few more items, quickly throwing clothes into a garbage bag, then they came downstairs and braved the cold again.

As the questions began flying, Carlos answered that they were staying with friends and asked them to respect their privacy.

Joe stepped forward and faced them. "Please. You don't get it, do you? My wife didn't ask for all this. She's a gentle soul. She did what she had to do. She had vascular surgery a month ago. She's a new mother. Can't you leave us alone? We may never be able to come home. We want to come home."

A few reporters looked ashamed and fell silent.

Carlos put his arm around Joe's shoulder and hefted his share of the load. He led the younger man to his car, and watched the rearview mirror carefully to evade followers. Once he was confident they were in the clear, he drove back to his dad's house.

"I could have used you in uniform, Papá, but if they'd recognized you, it would have led them here. What a mess. The stupid landlord even put up a sign!" Carlos said.

Martha and Candy looked at Joe. "Yep, it was bad. 'Home of Columbus' hometown hero.'"

"How can we ever go home?" Martha said.

"No problema here. Stay as long as you need to," Rod said. But he turned and muttered to himself, "Maybe a little problem."

Carlos grinned. "Got it bad, do ya, Papá?" he whispered.

"I want to go home," Candy said. "Not that you aren't wonderful to us."

"I told Joe every woman wants her nest for her bambino."

"I paid the old coot his rent and told him if he didn't want gawkers, he needs to take the sign down."

Martha swiped her hands together. "Well, nothing for it. We'll pray and make do, as long as we don't wear out the Rodriguez's hospitality." Taking the child by the hand, she said, "Now, Consuela, let me take your measurements. Stand here on this stool." She lifted her up, tickling her a bit. When she giggled, Martha tousled her black curls

When Martha finished, Carlos told his daughter they needed to go home, the baby would be awake now. "Won't Mamá be happy Miss Martha is making your costume?"

"And I am happy Abuelo is not sick. But you won't get your star, Abuelo, because you missed a Sunday."

"Ah, but we had an injury. Did you see poor Joe's face?"

"I heard about it on the drive," Carlos said, "but he said you were able to get her some reassurance. Where is Candy?"

"She and Mérida are upstairs, giggling like schoolgirls," Martha said.

"Isn't that what they are?" Carlos said. "Maybe this family is just what Candy needs. She's had to grow up too fast."

They watched Martha cutting the material on the dining room table. She didn't need a pattern. She used her measuring tape and snipped confidently, pinning here and there. He could hear the sound of the scissors, and thought perhaps he heard her hum—a contented sound.

Rod tossed Joe a Coke. "Let's see if we can catch the last of the game."

"We need to go. Come, Preciosa." Carlos stretched out his hand to his daughter. After hugs and more hugs for Abuelo, Consuela ran back to throw her arms around Martha one last time and tell her thank you, before they left.

Circling Jericho's Walls

After supper, the kids went upstairs. "I could put the baby in another room to give them some privacy," Rod said.

"You are too good to us, and your children have been nice. Carlos brought a Pack and Play for them, and he helped Joe today. I can't believe Mérida is giving up her days off to drive Candy to Mississippi!"

"She is a kind and generous girl, like her mamá."

"You loved her very much. How long were you married?"

"Twenty-two years."

"And she's been gone ten years? You don't look old enough."

"I'm not that old. We married when we were eighteen."

"I had Joe when I was eighteen."

Rod shook his head, smiling. "Ah, the hormones when we are young."

"Not for me—Scooter Long was dashing, but I wanted to escape home. I was the only child of older parents. I was born when my father was forty-nine, and my mother was forty-six. They were poor—made most of their cash money off moonshine and lived off the land, growing food and killing meat. They had no love in their hearts for a child, so I fell prey to the first man who put his hand up my skirt. I thought abuse was the way everyone lived."

"Is that the way it would be with us—me fifty, you forty-six?"

"Rod, I am too old."

"You are forty-six! That's not old."

"I had a hysterectomy after the fifth miscarriage. The only reason I carried Joe was Scooter got hurt on the job. He was up and around six months later, after Joe was born. He made sure we had no more babies. I lived with abuse all my life. I'm tired. I'll make it on my own. I'm content with my life."

"You have faith. I have faith. You deserve to be loved. We could make it work."

"Don't even go there, Rod. You are a good, decent, and loving man. I don't know how to love, and I really don't want to learn."

Rod's tender brown eyes swam. "Marta, you are the most loving person I know." When she shook her head, he continued. "You provided a home and protection for your son all his life. You worked and sacrificed to feed and clothe him. Then this poor broken girl comes into your life and you give her the mother she's never had. That's the love of God, shed abroad in your heart."

"That's different, loving your children, and Eddie is my life. But you're speaking of the love of a man with a woman. That takes trust. I have no trust."

"I will teach you."

She stood and raised her hand. "Please don't."

Rod watched her climb the stairs as if she was dragging a hundred-pound sack. A child of moonshiners, he would never have believed that. But she had told him she didn't live in that cabin in the hills. She spent her long, lonely childhood devouring books, walking to the library and sitting there for hours, afraid to take them home because the one she did carry home was used as kindling to start the fire. The librarian had a special shelf below her desk where Martha's books were kept. By the time she graduated high school, the kids ridiculed her because she had shed most of the dialect, at least the poor grammar, though she still spoke with a soft drawl. Well-read, she adopted the language of the friends of her childhood: Ivanhoe, Jane Eyre, Jo, Amy and the rest of the *Little Women*. She was alone, and she counted on no one, but it was how she survived.

Rod Rodriguez wondered how people could even be intact after the kind of abuse Martha and Candy had suffered, but he was determined. God had brought her to him, the way He had brought Joe to Candy, and by His Spirit these two wounded women would learn to trust. He was more a man of action than a man of prayer, but that night he spent a long time on his knees.

The next morning, he dropped Martha off at work, and Juan came by to take Joe to the trade school. It was an investment in his construction company, he told his father. He needed a good electrician; during the week, Joe went to the construction site after he finished class and earned wages. Juan brought him home.

Rod encouraged Mérida to come over in the afternoons after class, and she and Candy cooked dinner.

Mérida Grows Up

Mérida and Juan developed a new appreciation for their father, watching him with the young couple. Carlos told Juan about the small apartment and the used furnishings he saw. But his sister filled him in when she returned home from Mississippi.

First, she and Candy visited her mother in the nursing home. She was sallow, with the browned skin of a heavy smoker and the yellow cast of a heavy drinker. When Candy's mom saw Mérida, she called her a wetback and ridiculed Candy for her friends. Candy told her mother about the love of her Christian friends, and that she claimed Mérida as a sister. When her mother wanted to see Eddie, Mérida shuddered, but Candy went to the nurses' station where he slept in his car seat. Her mother showed some signs of connection, but her comment was the baby looked like her beloved Les, and her rheumy eyes swam with tears.

Mérida took a deep breath, watching her friend's struggle. She carried Eddie to the lobby and waited until Candy trudged into the waiting area and, with a shrug, said she was ready to go. She'd told her mother about Jesus and begged her to accept Him, which was all she could do. Mérida drove out to the trailer, where they found a pitiful stack of Candy's belongings in a charred pit in the back yard. The ground was parched and barren, not a sign of green anywhere.

The landlord confronted them about back rent—as if anyone paid money to live in that sty! Mérida held Eddie while Candy climbed the broken stairs and went inside. She could smell the fetid odors from the yard and walked the baby back to the car. Candy emerged from the nasty place she had called home, clutching two items: a locket of her grandmother's, and a photo she'd found of her father. Mérida wouldn't cry—by God, if Candy wasn't crying, she wouldn't!

"I guess this is all I have of my sorry life, Mer," Candy said. "I hate you saw it. I can't believe you've done this for me. You're a good friend."

"Like you told your mother, we're sisters. And I hope soon Papá and Martha will make us a real family."

"Martha says she's content the way she is. She had as bad a childhood as I did—although her sexual abuse didn't start until after she was married. Her parents beat her, though."

"How did you do it, Candy? Survive that, I mean."

"I didn't know any other way. At first it was school; I loved school, and did well. But after he started in on me, I made bad grades. I was two grades behind when I got to Hope House." She chuckled and leaned her head back on the seat. "One of the girls, Missy O'Malley, made me her pet project. She drummed all the bad grammar out of me, and taught me all I needed to get my GED. I hope you meet her someday."

Mérida looked over at her and wrinkled her nose. "We're getting you back to the motel—sorry, Kid, you stink."

Candy laughed then. "Between all the urine and Lysol at the nursing home and the rot and filth at the trailer, I could use a bath. I don't even want to touch Eddie until I get cleaned up."

"I'll try to hold him off, but he was nuzzling in the worst way. I gave him his pacifier. Hungry, huh Buddy?" Mérida caught his eye in the rearview mirror, and he gave her a toothless grin. "He is such a sweetie! Candy, don't listen to her. He doesn't look like Lester. He's the spitting image of you. He has your smoky grey eyes, the dimple in your chin, your elegant nose..."

Candy snorted. "My big old honker?"

Mérida slapped at her. "You have a beautiful nose. My nose is like the Maya Indians, broad and flat. I would kill to have your nose." She pulled into their motel. "You have a key; go inside. I'll get Eddie."

Mérida ordered pizza delivered to their room—Candy was too drained to go anywhere. Soon after she showered, it arrived. The girls sat cross-legged on the bed, watching a movie and giving Eddie lots of attention.

"I wish I could talk to Joe," Candy said.

"Papá wouldn't mind if you reversed the charges," Mérida said.

"Joe would. You guys have done so much for us, and he's proud."

"He is a good man, Candy. A good papá for Eddie."

"He is. I get scared sometimes. I don't want Eddie to be like Lester. I asked Beth and John if he'd have bad genes, or something."

Mérida caught her hand and squeezed it. "What did they say?"

"They told me he would be the way he is raised. He'll grow up with love; Joe and Martha adore him. I hope...I hope he'll be a good man. I don't want him to know about Lester. Joe married me before he was born so he could put his name on the birth certificate. I hope, if he does find out, that he doesn't hate me, and that he knows Joe is his daddy."

"He will. He'll grow up to be like Joe."

The girls went to bed; a 10-hour trip turned into a much longer one with a baby, and they wanted to start early in the morning.

They arrived home late Sunday afternoon. Martha had a pile of costumes in the making. Once the church ladies had seen Consuela's outfit, Martha was persuaded to make new ones for the entire angel choir. Carlos, Rod and Joe were talking in the dining room, but as soon as Joe saw his family, he was out of there. Martha excused him with a wave of her hand and a broad smile, and the couple took their son and went upstairs.

Mérida sank on the couch between her father and her brother. "Oh, Papá, you can't believe—I went to hell. That trailer..." She described the filth and the odor. "Candy came out with a tissue over her nose. I could hardly stand to be in the car with her, and I wouldn't let her hold Eddie until she bathed."

"Did you meet her mother?" Martha asked.

The young woman's black eyes snapped. "Ignorant woman called me a wetback! That's the only time Candy almost lost it. She put her arm around me and said I was the sister she never had. I walked out of the room."

"Where was Eddie?"

"He was asleep at the nurses' station, but he woke up when she took him in to see her mother. She asked me to come, so I kept my mouth shut, and that's not easy for me! That woman said he looked like Lester, and she went on and on about how he was dead now. Eddie looks like Candy, and I told her so."

Rod drew his daughter into his arms. "You did well, daughter, and I'm very proud of you."

"Papá, thank you for our home. Thank you for being my papá. I never dreamed anyone could live like that—even dogs live better than that."

"Papá grew up poor, Mer," Carlos said.

"Si, we were poor, but nothing like that. Mamá and Papá loved us, treasured us, and told us we were valuable because we belonged to God. Sometimes our bellies longed for food, and our house had a dirt floor, but Mamá was clean, and we were washed every day. She went to the pump and hauled buckets of water, and when we were old enough, we hauled them too. Sometimes she scrubbed so hard I thought she was trying to make us white, like the gringos."

Carlos and Mérida laughed, and Martha smiled.

"You see stuff like that all the time, Papá," Carlos said.

"I do—the drug dens, the meth labs, the poor, bruised and broken children."

"That's why you work with the boys' club, isn't it?" Mérida asked.

Martha knew several nights a week he came home late, telling her he volunteered as a mentor for boys his church served. She had gone to church with him that morning, she and Joe, and many young boys clung to him. He was a wondrous man, this gentle policeman who loved all children, his own and the outcast.

"Maybe I should see this boys' club. Are women allowed?"

"We give the boys a good meal, and we always need cooks—and the boys' clothes always need to be mended," Rod said. "Tuesday night, maybe—if you aren't too tired. How much of this sewing do you have?" He came and stood behind her, daring to touch her shoulders, massaging the muscles that had bent over the sewing machine all day and now took on more at night.

"This is my gift to Jesus for Easter. Sewing is easy for me. It is a small gift for all He's done for me. If I finish, tomorrow night, we can take them in."

"Papá, I've been thinking," Carlos said.

"That's dangerous." His father teased. "What?"

"That rundown carriage shed in the back of our house—I could have it fixed up and rent it to the Longs. The apartment they're in is not much better than that, as it is, and it's bigger."

"Next weekend we'll do a walk-through."

"You've done enough for us! We need to get out of your hair," Martha said.

"Ah, Marta, I like having you in my hair." He tugged on a lock of her hair before he walked his son to the door. "Mérida, are you ready to go home? Let Carlos get you to your car."

"'Night, Papá, te amo." She stood on tiptoe to kiss his cheek.

"You are a good girl."

"Gracias, Papá."

Mutual Respect

"You did a good job with that girl, and Juan, too," Martha said after the door closed behind them.

"They had a good start, and my mamá was here to help. You raised Joe all by yourself. *You* are the hero, in my book."

"You have a lack of heroes in your book." Martha looked away from the tenderness in his eyes. She started to go upstairs, but heard a burst of laughter from Joe and Candy's bedroom. "Perhaps another cup of coffee?"

"They seem happy. Joe is good for my Juan. He has helped him with his business, and they are getting close. They laugh a lot," Rod said.

"Juan is good for him. Joe's had too little laughter in his life."

"You, too, I think."

She took a deep breath. "Yes, me, too."

"Then we should have fun, yes?" Rod went over to the stereo, put on some salsa music, and said, "I will teach you."

"Oh, for heaven's sake!" she protested, but he caught her in his arms and spun her around the room until she gasped, laughing. "Joe, we were, uh…"

"Having fun. Come see your grandson, he's trying to roll over."

Martha and Rod trailed after him, peeking at Eddie, lying on his back and pulling his feet, as if that would get him on his tummy. Hearing them laugh, he craned his neck and plopped over. He was amazed at himself.

"Try it again, Little Man." Joe rolled him back. At first he was frustrated; then he remembered what had worked. He turned his head over, and his torso followed. He pushed himself up on his arms, beaming.

Rod chuckled. "Rover, roll over." Martha punched his arm, and he draped it over her shoulder. "He is a smart kid."

"Definitely brilliant," she agreed. "We were wondering about supper. Do you want anything?"

"I'll help you, Mom." Candy felt under the bed for her shoes, and they went to the kitchen together.

"She couldn't have made it without Mérida, Rod," Joe said as they followed. "It was a sorry mess."

"Mérida was shocked, and very sad," Rod told him. "The prison records said they had a meth lab in the trailer. Candy got out just in time."

Joe let out his breath slowly. "Thank God for that. By the way, I'm rooting for you—with Mom. Candy and I are praying for her. She's not hard, Rod, she's twice burnt."

"I know. I'm a patient man."

"She's worth it. Don't give up."

"I won't. God put her in a tender trap when she had to stay under my roof." Rod winked and threw his arm around Joe. He felt the young man stiffen before he relaxed in the light embrace. "Maybe you are worth it, too—and I know Candy is. Mérida said she never saw such faith and courage."

"She's worn out. We'll eat and go to bed early."

"For more reasons than one, eh?" Rod winked again when Joe blushed. "Don't mind me, I'm jealous!"

"What are you two guys up to?" Martha asked, eyeing them suspiciously.

"Guy talk, Mom, you don't want to know."

"Scrambled eggs and bacon?" she asked.

"I have jalapeños diced in a baggie."

Martha grimaced. "Two batches, bacon and toast, coming up." She walked into the kitchen. "Did you hear, Candy? He wants jalapeños in his eggs!"

"Get used to it, Mom." Martha put her hand on her hip and glared at her daughter-in-law. "Joe saw you dancing. You were having fun; admit it!" Martha turned away, checking the bacon and putting more bread in the toaster.

Candy looked around the table. Joe and Rod were laughing and teasing each other. Martha was smiling and shaking her head. Eddie was screaming delightedly. This was what families did. And when she yawned, everyone noticed and cared, and hustled her up to bed. Joe settled her in a tub with a cup of tea and played with Eddie while she soaked. She nursed the baby, and her husband tucked her in bed.

"You sleep, but I might wake you up later."

"Better do it carefully," she said. He laughed and dropped a kiss on her forehead. She'd thought she would cry all night and relive that horrible weekend, but echoes of laughter rang in her head instead, as she drifted off. She fell asleep quickly and slept soundly while Joe sat in a chair, studying his textbook.

Rod's Patience

Rod helped Martha with the dishes, then they moved into the living room. She went to the sewing machine. "Don't you want to rest?"

"I only have a few more. If I do one tonight, I can finish tomorrow night and go with you to the boys' club on Tuesday."

"Promise? Only if you're not too tired."

She had never imagined such a thoughtful man.

Rod caught that look, and it lifted his heart. Picking up his Bible, he read for a while, then he leaned his head back, praying silently. The woman made him pray! How he wanted her, he thought. He wanted her companionship, her wisdom, her happiness. He wanted her to lie beside him at night, and wake up with him in the morning. He didn't want to be alone anymore, but he didn't want to be with just anyone. He wanted this certain someone, this strong, lovely creature with eyes like mist on the mountain.

Martha stood. "What are you smiling at?"

"I am thinking of how your eyes look like mist on the mountain."

"Why do they call you Rod?"

"Too many Marios at work. Come sit by me."

To his surprise, she did, and when he laced her fingers, she didn't pull away. Progress.

"I owe you too much."

"You owe me nothing. I'm happy you're here."

"Joe has never leaned on a man before, never enjoyed an older man. And Candy adores you! Even Eddie lights up when he sees you."

"What about you, Marta? Do you enjoy me? Light up when you see me? Adore me?"

"Don't get ahead of yourself, but I am...fond of you."

"Fond."

"Yes, I like you, and I feel...comfortable here."

"That is good, Marta. I don't say your name right."

"Marta is good. I like that; it's your name for me."

He smiled and looked into her eyes. Before she was aware what he intended, he brushed a quick kiss across her lips. He rose, not pushing his luck, and snapped off the light. They walked wordlessly up the stairs, and when they stopped outside her bedroom, he gently ran his knuckles down the side of her face.

"Goodnight, beautiful Marta."

She said goodnight quietly, but when she went inside and closed the door, she leaned against it, feeling his soothing caress and the gentle brush of his lips on hers. She touched her lips and felt his gentle pressure. She touched her face, and she was not afraid. That was a good thing.

Tuesday morning, Rod heard singing in his kitchen. His step quickened, and he entered the room, taking in Martha's graceful movements as she reached for two mugs. The coffee pot was already gurgling, and the aroma of brewing coffee tantalized his nose. She turned, startled when she saw him, and raised her hand to her mouth.

"I hope you don't mind," she said. "I've been reading, and wanted some."

"Of course not—it's pleasant to smell coffee. It makes it easier to get up." He opened the refrigerator to reach for the cream, and she set the steaming mugs on the table. He noticed she didn't seem as ill-at-ease, and he was glad he hadn't alarmed her last night.

Rod lifted his cup. "Delicioso. Very good."

"Did I make it strong enough?"

"Perfect." After they chatted, he went across the family room to his study, leaving the door open, and reached for his Bible. When she hovered near the doorway, he waved her in. Usually Rod closed the door when he was having time with the Lord, but he welcomed her presence. She wasn't chatty. She was serene, and she quieted him.

She settled in a chair, and the pages of her own Bible rustled. She laid her hand on the open Bible and studied him.

He felt her eyes. "What are you reading?"

"I'm doing a word search on fear," she said. "'God has not given us a spirit of fear,'" she quoted. "Fear torments us. It isn't of God."

"You have fear?"

"I do—it's eased since Scooter died, but my lack of trust is fear. If a teenage girl can confront her fears and overcome them, a grown woman surely should be able to, don't you think? Look at Candy—all she's been through, and she is radiant!"

"What do you fear?"

"I fear being dependent. I have only counted on myself since I was a child—and Joe, once he got older. I fear rejection: ever since I was a little girl, no one wanted me. I fear a man will hurt me. I have never had anyone to trust, and I fear being abandoned."

God, what do I say to Your daughter? "And God? Will He forsake you, too?"

"God is faithful. He will never leave me or forsake me."

"What about one of His servants who loves Him very much?" *And who loves you very much, beautiful Marta.*

Her eyes brightened. "Pray for me, Mario."

He crossed the room and took her hands, leading her to the small two-seat sofa in his office. They sat side by side.

"Candy wanted to buy a house," she said in a few moments. "Thank you for helping them. It would have been too much for Joe. He has to finish his schooling. I'm glad he doesn't have that pressure."

"He fell behind with her surgery, but he is catching up. We'll pray for them, but first we will ask God to take away your fear." Rod didn't tell her about Carlos's plan, because he had serious doubts that old carriage house could be repaired and safe. They prayed, and when she looked at him, those grey eyes didn't turn away. She met his tender glance, seeming to soak it in.

"You are a good man."

"And now you must pray for me. I have a meeting this morning, and I think a promotion."

"That's good, isn't it?"

"I always said I would quit when police work was no longer fun. To sit behind a desk and push papers is not fun."

"But it is safer." Martha looked away, and her voice dropped. He strained to catch her words. "I could not bear it, if anything should happen to you." His heart thumped in his chest. She looked up. "You will be a leader of men. You can teach them to be safe. That's important."

"You've given me a new perspective—and a reason to take this job." She blushed, but began to pray firmly for his direction, tightening her grip on his hands.

Gently pulling them out of her grasp, he said, "And now we must get moving or we'll be late, no?"

Rod called Martha as soon as he knew. He'd taken the job. They chatted briefly and at quitting time, Rod showed up at the laundry.

"What are you doing here?"

"I took off early so we could go celebrate. Hungry?"

"Don't we feed the boys at the church"?"

"I'm not in the mood for hot dogs. I know a nice place."

"Let's go to the cantina."

"You like that place?"

"It has good memories." Martha called out a goodnight to her coworker.

Rod opened the door for her. He helped her into his truck out front. They drove to the Mexican restaurant and ate, laughing and talking easily. She told him she'd thanked God to hear he'd gotten the job, and she knew he'd be a good influence on the younger men. Remembering their first time here, Rod rejoiced in her ease with him, with them. Progress. Reluctantly he stood. It was time to go. When he touched her waist, she didn't pull away.

As soon as they came into the church building, Rod was swarmed, and when the bus pulled in, another group of boys ran up to him. Laughing he hugged one, pulled on the bill of a ball cap of another, and drew yet a third boy into an embrace. "Boys, we have a guest. Say good evening to Mrs. Long."

Some of the boys had met her on Sunday. They all mumbled something. "She's pretty, Officer Rod. Is she your girlfriend?" one asked.

"From your lips to God's ears, Kid." He winked at Martha. "Come. I'll introduce you to the other ladies." But Martha needed no introduction; her angel costumes preceded her. She carried the remaining ones in her arms. She joined the women in the kitchen as they prepared macaroni and cheese and ham sandwiches.

Rod watched Martha help with serving. She moved among the boys, talking about families and homework, and she had fine-tuned radar for the at-risk children. She squatted beside one boy's chair, and Rod was shocked to see the shy boy bloom under her warm sun. Martha gave him a light squeeze, and his arms surrounded her neck as he clung to her.

Rod checked on her several times and heard the ladies chatting about people in the kitchen. They looked at him and back to her when he popped in. He had good friends at his church, and she was under inspection, but when they left, they hugged her, telling her what a big help she was and begging her to come back.

"What did you think?" Rod asked.

"It was fun. It's a nice group of ladies."

"You'll come back?"

"If you want."

"Marta, you should know by now, I never want you out of my sight." He waiting for her reaction. Her lips curved into her quiet smile, and he let go of the breath he'd been holding. When they got home, she told Candy and Joe all about their evening. Rod had never seen her so animated—in fact, neither had Joe.

Joe came back downstairs after Candy and Eddie went to bed. He had a test tomorrow, and he had to do well or he'd be put back. He turned on another light in the family room.

Rod was in his office, and he looked up. After he straightened some papers, he turned off his lamp, and came into the living room. "Studying?" he asked, and Joe explained his dilemma. "You'll do fine, Son. Let's pray about it."

They did, and Joe thanked him. "It's a big responsibility; I think of those two up there. I want to give them the sun and the moon, but I must keep a roof over their head, you know?"

"I had seven, remember, and Maria. Yes, it's a responsibility. Your mother and Candy have never had anyone they could count on."

"I've never seen Mom like she was tonight. She's happy, and when you touch her, she doesn't look like she wants to run away. Candy and I are praying for you."

"We're making progress."

"You don't know the half of it!" Joe said. "I remember many trips to the hospital, after the beatings. I waited for her, and she told me not to answer any questions. I sat in the hard plastic chairs for hours, swinging my feet against the legs to keep awake. She is the bravest woman I know."

"She and Candy," Rod replied.

"And Candy—the first time I saw her I knew she'd had tough times, and she did, but Mérida told me about the trailer. It was worse than I imagined."

"After she left, they set up a meth lab in there," Rod told him.

Joe shuddered and picked up his book. After cautioning him not to stay up too late, Rod patted his back and left.

Joe came home the next evening on cloud nine. "I had the highest grade in the class, Rod. Thanks for your prayers."

"I told you, Joe. You're so smart!" Candy exclaimed, throwing her arms around him.

"Shall we play hooky from church and go out to celebrate?" Rod asked.

Martha slipped her arm through his and told them he'd gotten a promotion. Joe covered his smile and winked at Rod. Candy gave him a thumbs-up behind Martha's back. The family—that's how Rod thought of them now—went to a nice restaurant. He'd gotten a pay raise, after all.

The wives went to the ladies' room, taking Eddie to change him.

"Do you know what Carlos is doing?" Joe asked Rod.

"Don't get your hopes up, Kid; that building is about to fall in," Rod cautioned, adding, "In God's time. Your mother and I are praying about that. Young families should have a home of their own—of course, you know I want to marry Marta. As soon as she agrees, she will live with me."

Joe responded, "You're right. It's best not to get Candy's hopes up. She wants a house in the worst way." Seeing the women approach the table, he quickly added, "And we are praying with you." He stood and held Candy's chair. Eddie reached for him.

"What are we praying for?" she asked.

"You know."

Rod held Martha's chair, and briefly rested his hands on her shoulders. He felt a tremor but it wasn't an unpleasant one. He squeezed gently. Progress.

Moving

Joe did have hope for the carriage house, because he knew more than Rod did. He and Juan had already set new support beams. But he kept confidence with Juan and Carlos, knowing they wanted to surprise him. He and Juan worked half the day, lifting those beams into place.

Joe had two days off while his instructor remediated much of the class. They continued working, and didn't breathe a word to their parents. Juan brought his entire crew over to the Carriage House, and work advanced rapidly. Carlos stopped by every evening, and ordered the appliances Friday. The kitchen would be the last thing completed, but he assured Joe they could eat with them until it was ready.

"It'll be a bit rough, but we'll get the living room done and move your things from the apartment next week."

"I'll start paying you rent then."

"Nonsense. You aren't paying rent to live in a construction site. Let's get it finished before we talk about that. Let me go change, and I'll give you a hand. Papá's going to be surprised. You guys have made a lot of progress."

Joe told the brothers what their father had said about the Carriage House, and they laughed.

Saturday, after Rod took Martha to work, Joe took Candy to see the work in progress behind Carlos's large home.

Rod dropped by, and he was surprised to find it clean and the renovations well under way. Carlos, his daughter, Alexandra, and his older son, Marco, were in work clothes, sanding, sweeping, and helping.

Joe took Candy's hand, explaining that Carlos would rent this home to them, if she liked it. Candy's smoky eyes overflowed, but he had learned to discern the difference between happy tears and sad ones, and he drew her into his arms.

"It's bigger than the apartment, and Carlos says Eddie can play in the yard—it's fenced securely for his kids. Do you like it? Come see the kitchen. We still have a lot to do in there."

Candy followed him in, trailing her hands over woodwork and stepping over stacks of lumber. She turned around in the kitchen. "But we don't have a stove or refrigerator."

"Carlos says that's the landlord's responsibility. He's already ordered them. We're building a counter here."

"He would do this for us? All this expense?"

"He's been planning to fix it up for some time. Don't you like it? Isn't it great?"

"We don't have enough furniture," Candy said.

Rod was on a ladder, painting nearby. Overhearing, he assured her he had furniture stored from the kids' apartments, if she didn't mind furnishing in "early attic."

"Why are you doing all this for us?" Candy asked.

"Haven't you ever heard when you save a person's life you are responsible for him?" He climbed down and took her by the hand. "Besides, Carlos wants to help me win Marta's hand."

"How's that going, Papá?" his oldest son asked as he came into the kitchen with another bucket of paint.

"Progress—I'm making some headway," he replied. "Maybe she won't move in with you. How long do you think this will take?"

"Juan estimates it'll take another six weeks, but they could store their furniture by the end of the next week and camp out in two. In that timeframe, we could get them out of the apartment before the next month's rent is due."

"That might be pushing it for Marta," his father said.

Juan winked. "We can drag our feet on the downstairs bedroom and leave her at your house a while longer."

"She wouldn't stay without a chaperone," Joe said, and Rod agreed. "Where's Candy?" Joe said, looking around.

Carlos pointed out the window. Candy was talking to his wife, Conchesca, sitting on a swing with Eddie on her lap, gently moving back and forth. Consuela was hanging on to her mother's hand, begging Candy to move today. The girl's mother said something, and Candy threw her head back and laughed.

"I've ever seen her laugh like that," Joe said.

"Conchesca would make a statue laugh. She made me laugh, and I was the most driven workaholic ever. She joined my firm, and I haven't stopped laughing since," Carlos said, beaming affectionately at his wife. She waved and tucked her arm under Candy's, pulling her to the big house.

"Let's get to this," Rod said, stripping off his shirt. Soon the others arrived, and men worked until it was time to get Martha. Rod was mortified to pick her up in his sweaty tee shirt, but they assured him he was quite macho looking. He swatted at Juan and took off with a smile.

Martha looked at him when she got in his truck, and asked him what he'd been doing. He winked and told her he would show her. "Where are we going?" she asked when he drove an unfamiliar route.

"To Carlos's place, where my boys have gathered to work. They are making renovations. No more questions. You'll see." They pulled up in front of an elegant old mansion painted Williamsburg green, in an elite section of Columbus. Dark shutters framed the beveled glass windows. An historical marker in the yard proclaimed the house was built in 1894.

"Oh my, how lovely!" she exclaimed. "But it looks renovated already."

He opened her door and offered his hand. When she took it, he tucked hers under his arm and walked her around the house. He pushed open black iron gates leading to the driveway in back and pointed. Like ants, his boys swarmed around the carriage house. Tomás and Ricardo were on ladders, painting and laughing, white teeth flashing against brown skin. Carlos and Juan were hauling lumber inside the open front door.

"Carlos is fixing up the old Carriage House for the Long family," he announced. "Come see." As he pulled her along, he told her they hoped to have it ready before their next rent was due, and that Conchesca was getting along famously with Candy. Joe and Juan had been working on it all week. When she lingered, he paused.

"Are we too much? My family can be overwhelming. Please, look. Joe and Candy are happy." He led her into the large hallway. "This will be a bedroom." He pointed to the left. "Upstairs will be two bedrooms. The kitchen is straight ahead. Eddie will have a fenced yard to play in." He walked ahead of her to the spacious kitchen, which was gutted, but she could see the dining alcove, with big bay windows looking out over a lawn. Hearing her sniff, he looked around in alarm.

He quickly assured her Carlos had wanted to renovate the derelict old building ever since they'd moved in. "It still needs work, but it'll be nice. You'll see, Marta. Let me show you the paints."

She stood in front of the bay window in the kitchen, overlooking the yard, her hand over her mouth. She turned in a circle. "I've never lived in such a place," and then, to his surprise, she flung her arms around his neck and buried her face in his sweaty shirt.

"I am dirty and stinky," he protested, but she lifted her beautiful grey eyes and looked into his dark ones.

"You're a wonderful man, with an incredible family. Thank you."

"I don't want you to live here, Marta."

"You said we could be here before the next rent was due…"

"Joe and Candy can live here. You, I want with me, in my house. Marta, please say yes. I'll wait until you trust me—you can stay in the guest room if you aren't ready, but say you'll marry me."

In response, she lifted her face. He framed her cheeks with his hands and slowly lowered his mouth to hers. Her response was beyond his wildest dreams, and he put his arms around her and drew her close, sweat, sawdust and all. She leaned into him. They neither saw nor heard the boys back down the hall.

Romance in the Air

"That was hot, Carlos!" Juan whispered. Joe came up, and they told him not to go in the kitchen because Martha and their father were kissing—most passionately.

Joe pumped his fist. The three of them moved to the front of the house and slapped each other on the back. Seeing them through the window, Tomás clamored down the ladder and demanded to know what was up. He raced up the ladder and loudly whispered to Ricardo, "Guess what Papá and Martha are doing? Kissing, that's what, and Carlos says it's hot and heavy."

Seeing Candy approach, Joe caught her, whirling her around until she made him put her down, laughing and demanding to know what was going on. The men crowded around her, detailing the story, and she jumped up and down.

"I came to tell you supper is ready."

"Man, Papá is devouring your mamá, Joe," Juan teased.

"Juan, that's his mamá," Carlos cautioned.

"It's a good thing. Rod is good for her," Joe said.

The brothers stared at him. "What?"

"He is good for her?" Carlos asked.

"You bet. I've never seen her this happy."

They exchanged glances. "Papá hasn't been this happy since Mamá got sick."

"I've never seen Mom happy. She was pleased with Candy and me, and when Eddie was born, but always a sadness lurked in her eyes."

Juan, who was facing the door, nudged with his elbow. "Shh—here they come. Look busy." He grabbed a tool box and banged it into Joe's knee. Joe hollered and hopped around. Ricardo and Tomás fell on the ground, laughing. Carlos was holding his sides, and Candy had tears running down her cheeks.

"You boys are being foolish."

"Yes, Papá," they chorused, trying vainly to sober up.

"We have something important to tell you," Rod said.

"Oh?" Carlos said.

"Whatever could that be, Papá?" Juan asked innocently, and then they all cracked up again.

A flush mounted on Martha's cheek. She put her hands on her hips and glared around the circle. "You were spying on us."

"Yes, Ma'am," Carlos said, pulling her into a hug. "And let me be the first to congratulate you. We are truly happy, Martha."

Candy put her arm around her mother-in-law and tugged her toward the big house. "Supper is on, Mom. Come, tell us all about it."

Juan whispered to Tomás, "She might want to leave off the R-rated part."

Thwack! Juan looked back and groaned, rubbing the side of his head. Rod was behind him. "Have some respect," he growled.

"Yes, Papá," Juan said, and Tomás started to laugh.

"Who knew you were such a stud, Papá?" Tomás said, and ran off.

Rod threw his hands in the air, muttering in Spanish. Martha walked back and took his hand. "They are funning with you, Mario. Your boys love you. They're happy for us."

"What is this 'funning with me,' Marta?"

"They tease you because they love you. and they're happy for you," Candy said. She slipped her arm around his waist and leaned against his shoulder.

The house was packed with children and spouses—a meeting of the family.

Rod walked over to his mother to hold her chair. He leaned to kiss her cheek. "Marta has agreed to marry me, Mamá."

"This is good, Mario, and soon," the old lady replied.

"Couldn't be too soon!" Juan said.

"When, Papá?" Carlos asked, shooting his younger brother a look.

"As soon as you have Candy and Joe in their new home, so let's eat and get back to work."

Rod took a side chair, waving Carlos to the head of his table. The family bowed for the blessing. Martha's hand sought his hand under the table, and he fought tears manfully. He brought her hand to his lips, and her sweet smile made his heart rejoice.

To move the romance along, in a week Rod, Juan, and Carlos used their trucks to move the Longs' pitiful collection of meager possessions into the large front room. It didn't even crowd the space. Juan and Carlos exchanged glances.

"The first time I went into that apartment—the night of the shooting—I was too busy to look around," Rod said. "I got to know them at the hospital, and this family is rich in love. When I visited Marta, I couldn't believe how poor they are. The two of them were struggling to make ends meet, to get Joe into school, and they opened their hearts to Candy, sharing what they had. Listening to Mérida, the apartment was the nicest place she'd lived."

Carlos cleared his throat. "We can scrounge stuff—you've got a lot of our college furniture stored upstairs, Papá."

"I told Candy we would furnish them in early attic," Rod replied.

"That about does it," Juan said. "Papá, we're on target. We'll have Joe and Candy in here in two weeks. Better plan that wedding." He winked. "If it's okay, I have a date tonight, so I'll be off."

"You, I don't mind. You are a man yet. Jacinta is pushing it."

"Papá, she is only twenty-five. Conchesca was twenty-six when we got married. Just because you and mom married at eighteen doesn't make twenty-five old." Carlos said. "And I'd rather have her single than with Jeffery. She came in one day and took off her sweater. I saw a large bruise; when she saw me looking, she covered it quickly and showed us a diamond bracelet he'd given her. He has given her lots of pretty gifts, but we hardly see her anymore, and I don't like it. Does she know about you and Martha?"

Rod frowned. "We ask her to dinner, and she doesn't come. Always, she has something to do. You are right, this does not look good." Rod climbed in his truck, and they said goodnight.

The carriage house was ready in two weeks; that Saturday morning, Rod and Martha were married, with all of their children and grandchildren present. Of course, the Rodriguez family filled the chapel. Rod talked them out of a reception, knowing Martha would be overwhelmed to have so much attention focused on them. Instead, they planned a housewarming for Joe and Candy, serving punch and sandwiches. When the younger couple had married, they'd had a small bridal shower at Hope House—but their friends were not in a position to give them much. Rod's children liberally showered them with matching silverware and a full set of china, towels, sheets, kitchenware, and decorative items for their home.

Jacinta was there, but she was nervous and in a hurry, and left early.

Rod caught Carlos's eye, and they shook their heads.

Martha hugged Candy as she helped her stack up all her new things. "Tomorrow, I will come back and help you put all this away." She and Rod left, lugging all the linens over to their house to wash because the laundry room wasn't finished at the carriage house.

Rod and Martha pulled away alone, leaving the couple in their new quarters. He glanced over to take a reading on his new wife. Was she anxious? She was quiet on the drive, but Martha was always quiet. She hadn't mentioned sleeping arrangements, and he wondered what she wanted. He was determined to be patient while he built her trust. They carried the laundry inside and sorted the sheets and towels, starting the darks first.

"Now, what would you like?" he asked. "Do you want supper?"

"I'm still full from the party," she said.

"Something to drink?" he asked.

"Are you hungry? Conchesca packed us plenty of food."

"I'm good, Marta. You were a beautiful bride. Where did you get the dress?"

"I made it."

"You have a gift."

"I like to sew; it's easy for me."

"You don't have to work. I have a nice salary. The house is paid for. We are comfortable, no?"

Martha looked at him with alarm. "I won't quit my job. I need my job."

"I'm saying you don't have to work."

"I do. I must. I will work."

"We need to get you a car then, so you won't have to ride the bus and walk."

"I don't need a car. I don't have a license. Why pay for two cars, insurance, upkeep, gas, and taxes? No!" She stood, paced, and wrung her hands.

Rod looked at her increasing agitation. "Come, sit. Whatever you want is fine, but I wanted to tell you that you don't have to work. You've worked all your life."

"I have. I've paid into Social Security since I was sixteen."

"So, you need to work to feel secure. I understand, but I promise I'll take care of you."

Martha looked around wildly.

"Marta, Marta," he whispered. "Come here, little bird. Don't fly away." He held out his hand.

She studied it for a moment, and then took it. He tugged her gently into his lap. "Keep your job, no car—but I'll teach you to drive so you can be more independent, no?"

"I'll wreck that big truck!"

He chuckled. "We will use Mérida's little car; it's in my name. Okay?"

She leaned against him and he kissed her hair, feeling her relax. He reached up and snapped off the lamp, and they sat in the waning light until the timer went off on the washing machine. While Martha put the darks in the dryer and loaded the towels into the washer, Rod made tea. He preferred coffee, but he thought tea might be more soothing this evening

When she sipped it, she looked over the edge of the cup. "You know I fell in love with your family, don't you?"

"That is not so flattering, I think."

She set her cup on the table and took his hand, bringing it to her lips. "And then I knew the family reflects the Papá, and I knew I was...safe."

Rod pulled her to his lap again, and she lifted her face to receive his kiss. He was hesitant, but she was responsive. When they broke apart, she suggested they go upstairs. She went into the hall bathroom, and he stifled a sigh as he walked to his bedroom. He heard her shower and took his own. He was leaning against the headboard trying to read, trying to pray, trying not to think, when he heard a timid knock.

"Come in."

The door opened, and she stood in a long pink gown, with dainty flowers about the collar and down the bodice. She didn't realize the hall light behind her revealed her lovely body.

His face lit up. "Do you want to sleep in here?"

Her eyes darted around. He went to the door, took her hand, and led her to the bed, turning down the covers on the empty side. She slipped under, and he covered her.

"We don't have to do anything you don't want to do, mi amor. I will wait. Her grey eyes sought his black ones, and she moved close to him, lowering her head to his chest. He stroked her arm.

Like a timid puppy, she inched closer.

Rod smiled and tucked his hand under her chin. "May I kiss you, Marta?"

Her light grey eyes had darkened. She nodded; when their lips met, she cried out a little—but it was a soft, welcoming sound. When they broke apart, she whispered, asking if he would turn out the light.

He did, wondering if she wanted to sleep now, knowing he wouldn't if she did, but she said no, and they did what lovers do.

Sometime toward morning, he moved against her and felt her stiffen. He reached over and turned on the bedside lamp.

She blinked. "What?"

"I didn't want to frighten you. I didn't want you to—what did Joe say? I don't want to go to work with a black eye."

Martha put her arm around his middle. "I would never hit you. Fighting made it worse. I never defended myself."

"I would never hurt you." His hands ran over her back. He had felt ridges on her skin earlier. "Marta?"

"Hmm?"

"Would you...would you mind if I saw?"

Martha had kept her nightgown on, allowing him to tug it up, but not off. She sat up, and turned her back, pulling it up to her shoulders.

Rod was horrified by the crisscross of welts and knotted scars. He sucked in his breath.

She covered her face with her hands. "I told you I was damaged. I am sorry."

"Why?"

"I'm ugly and broken."

"Mi amor," he whispered.

She felt wet droplets on her skin as he knelt behind her and tenderly kissed each one. His touch was gentle as spring rain, his lips traced her scars, and, when he was through, he smoothed her gown down and turned her, pulling her into his arms.

"I am sorry you suffered," he whispered, before kissing her silent tears.

"I always wondered about the passage in Proverbs, about the wondrous things, and the way of a man with a maiden. Last night I thought of that verse when you loved me. I never wanted a man's love. Now I do."

"May I love you again, Marta?" She simply smiled.

They were a little late to church, but slipped in the pew beside Joe and Candy.

Candy laced her mother-in-law's fingers with her own. "I can tell by your eyes it was good," she whispered.

"Like you promised. Thanks for letting me borrow your book." Martha reached for Rod's hand and felt safe when his strong brown fingers curved around hers.

Joe couldn't hear the whispers beside him, but he saw his mother's contented face and leaned forward to catch Rod's eye. Joe winked, and Rod smiled broadly.

The family went to the Carlos's house for lunch. Everyone carefully avoided mentioning Jacinta's absence, but Rod worried about his daughter and sent her a text. She replied she'd try to come by later.

After lunch, the ladies bustled around putting items away in the door-less linen closet, hanging the new towels in the completed bathroom upstairs, and washing all the dishes before arranging them on the shelves. Joe said they had the doors sanded and painted, and they would be mounted the next day, but it would be a while yet before the counter was complete. Meantime, they set the pots and pans on the ledge of the bay window.

"Joe," Candy said, looking out onto the lawn. "I've learned that it is better to wait upon the Lord." He had come to stand behind her, and she turned to put her arms around him. "This is a beautiful house! It's more than I hoped, better than I dreamed."

Rescuing Jacinta

Jacinta's dream was turning to a nightmare. Jeffery had become increasingly possessive and jealous. He refused to join the family, and kept her out too late to go by. He became angry when she wanted to be with her family, and he was increasingly insistent that she move in with him. She told him it was against her beliefs, and he ridiculed her, complaining she didn't love him. He knew where she was every moment of the day, and she didn't have any time to herself. She decided to seek out her Papá, to get his counsel. She took a personal leave day and drove to his precinct.

Rod rarely closed his office door, wanting to keep his finger on the pulse of the office, to hear what his men were talking about. He had completed the day's briefing when he heard welcoming sounds and looked up from his desk to see his daughter, trying to smile and joke with the guys. He walked out and took her by the arm, drawing her into his office and closing the door firmly behind him.

"Now you will tell me? Your Papá?"

"Sí, Papá." She was afraid, and told him what all the family already knew—Jeffery controlled her every movement, her every interaction.

"This is a very bad relationship." She ducked her head but nodded. "I will run some background checks on this man, this Jeffery, but you must break it off." Seeing her hesitation, he said, "I will go with you. Would you like that?"

She reached for his hand, and he took her in his arms as she wept.

They considered where she could go, because he knew where she lived and where she worked. Finally, she said she would go to Carlos, because Jeffery didn't like him and forbade her to go to his office.

"This man wouldn't allow you to go to your brother's work? This is not good. I will look for records on him. Then we will take you to Carlos." Rod booted up his computer, and within a few whirring moments, Jeffery's face popped up on the screen. He was divorced, more than once, and had several charges of domestic violence. He quickly helped her file a restraining order.

"But these papers do not keep you safe. I wish you to have a gun."

"Papá, I will not carry a gun! I hate violence. Nothing is ever solved with a gun."

"I have my Marta because Candy was brave enough to have a gun—and use it."

"I couldn't, Papá."

"I will get you pepper spray, but that is nothing to a man like that. We must get your clothes and move you into the house with Marta and me. Would you do that?"

She agreed. "But when will we tell him?"

"When are you supposed to see him?"

"He comes by the school every day when I get off."

"What does this man do for work?"

"He's a day trader. He works at home."

"I will take you to Carlos, and be there at the school when he comes. I will stand by your car and bring him to you. Carlos and I will help you tell him you want to break off this relationship. This is what you want, no?"

"Sí, Papá."

"You will not go back to him? Women do."

"I won't. I saw those charges on your screen."

"One of his wives was never found, Jacinta."

Her eyes grew round.

"Come, we will go."

When Jacinta got to her brother's office, she was trembling so hard that Conchesca took her into the kitchen and fixed her soothing tea while Rod filled Carlos in on what was happening. They agreed to end this today.

Jacinta tried to help with office tasks, but she was too jittery to accomplish anything. When her phone rang after school, she went pale. Carlos stood by her shoulder.

"It's him?" She nodded. "Don't answer," Carlos advised.

The phone rang again. Papá. "Yes? It's a dark blue BMW with tinted windows. Are you by my car?" She hung up and reached for her brother's hand. "He sees him. God, don't let anything happen."

"To Papá or to Jeffery?" Carlos asked, catching his wife's look.

"To anybody! How did this happen? I made a mess, didn't I? I should have listen to you, Hermano."

"We will be here for you, Jacinta."

After the longest twenty minutes of her life, she saw a blue BMW pull in with a police car behind it, blue lights flashing.

Carlos went to the front door and escorted their father, following Jeffery, inside. He led them to his office and closed the door.

Seeing Jacinta, Jeffery demanded to know what this was all about. "Are you arresting me?" He spun around to face Rod. "I will charge you with police brutality! Tell them, Jacinta. Tell them you love me."

Jacinta stood. "I want you to leave me alone. Don't call. Don't come by. I don't want to see you anymore."

"Who is making you do this?"

"No one is making her. She came to her papá for help. We have a restraining order against you. You are not to come near her, nor seek contact," Rod slapped the papers in his hand.

"I have done nothing to her! How can you do this?"

"On the basis of your past history."

"And I saw bruises, Papá," Carlos said.

"Is this true, Jacinta?" She nodded. "Often?"

"More recently, when I refused to...move in with him."

"Cohabit?"

"I didn't. I never...he wanted to, but it's not our way."

Rod almost chuckled. "Ah, Mr. Maloney, you have picked the wrong family to mess with. Now, leave us, all of us, alone, and do not make any attempt to contact her again. Is that clear?"

Shooting a furious look at Jacinta, calling her a filthy name, Jeffery stalked out of the office.

Rod advised Carlos to increase security around their building, add more cameras, and perhaps hire some watchmen. "I know some retired officers who would help with surveillance."

"Is he that dangerous?" Conchesca asked.

"He has multiple charges of domestic violence and one missing wife. Yes. He is an unstable man, and we must protect her. I'm taking her to my house, to Marta. Some of the boys will take her to her home to get her things later. She will not live alone."

"Dear God," Conchesca murmured.

After Jacinta took a few sick days, she went back to work, but Rod took his daughter every day and among the sons, someone picked her up, but it was Martha who healed her. Rod was amazed when she showed Jacinta her shameful scars and told her of her years of abuse, and how she almost died, encouraging her courageous step. She told Jacinta she wished she had been brave enough to leave, but Rod knew she had no family to support her. She had no one. They worked together in the kitchen; Jacinta taught her to make enchiladas and burritos, and she taught Jacinta to make barbeque and pinto beans.

One morning, on the way to work, Jacinta told her father she loved this quiet, gentle woman. "She is different from Mamá, but good for all of us—she and Joe and Candy. Mérida loves Candy."

"Candy has been good for Mérida, and Joe is good for Juan. God brought this family to us, and we are richer for it," Rod told his daughter.

"I love Martha. I wish I had been around during your romance."

"Ah, every day is a romance. She never knew love before."

"She's well-loved now, Papá."

"Sí. I love her."

"I don't know love. I was in love with love, but the Rodríguez men never lift a hand up against their wives."

"That is a great sin. God gives us women to cherish and protect."

"You've always done that, Papá. Why was I so foolish to fall for a man like that?"

"Do you hear from him?"

"No."

"I saw his car, but when I ran the plates, it was a new owner."

Jacinta's eyes filled. "Thank you, Papá, for helping me."

"This is what families do, no? Carlos, your big brother, watches after you."

Eventually, Jeffery seemed to disappear. Finally, Jacinta moved into her own place, in a gated community, but she was always a part of every gathering, and a frequent babysitter for her nieces and nephews.

Rod Long

Joe and Candy lived in the carriage house for years, and increased their family there. Conchesca's nanny added Eddie to her responsibilities. (Carlos added additional salary to her paycheck.) Candy finished beauty school and got a job in a mall franchise. Joe completed his electrician training and began a master course, still working for Juan. Juan had paid his tuition, and he'd agreed to work for him three years. They had no debt because the small reward paid Candy's school, so they decided to have another baby. If they had a girl, they would put her in the second bedroom upstairs and move downstairs, but the sonogram revealed another son.

"Mer," Candy whispered into the phone, "can you come get me?"

"What's wrong? You sound awful—are you in pain?"

"I hurt."

"Where?"

"My leg. Please come."

Mérida flew out of her office in Carlos's executive suite, hollering to Conchesca that she was getting Candy, and it sounded bad. She dialed her boyfriend on the way, telling him to meet her in the mall. He refused to walk into a beauty shop until she came to the door and dragged him by the hand. Sam looked at Candy, doubled over, her head on her knees.

"Hold on, Kid," he said, sweeping her in his arms. "My keys are in my pocket. We'll take my car, it's bigger."

Mérida sat in the back and Sam settled Candy on the seat, with her head in her friend's lap. Mérida wiped Candy's hair out of her face. "It's your bad leg?" Candy nodded. "Better take her to Wexner—that's where she had her surgery."

Sam pulled into the ER, and Mérida ran for a wheelchair. Candy was diagnosed with a blood clot and admitted before they could locate Joe on the work site. By the time he got there, Carlos, Conchesca, and Martha were crowded into her room.

Breathless, he ran to her side as the family parted. She had an IV in her arm, but by this time her pain had eased. She took his hand and whispered she was sorry.

The others filed out, Martha promising to stay with Eddie at the carriage house.

Joe was alarmed when the familiar vascular surgeon came in with a chart in his hand.

"I assume you want this baby, Mrs. Long."

Candy's dark grey eyes flared. "*Of course* I want this baby!"

"I remember you. I know you do. Now that I have your attention, I'm telling you that you cannot go back to work until after the birth. You have three more months?" She nodded. "Elastic stockings or no, you must be off your feet. Hopefully we can get you home in a few days, but you must keep your feet up. You have other children?"

"Eddie—remember the baby? He's five now, and in kindergarten. He stays with a sitter in the afternoons."

Joe looked at the doctor fearfully. "Her artery is okay?"

"She'll be fine. Her leg was terribly swollen, and she developed a clot. We have her on blood thinners, but we have to be careful of the pregnancy. Once the clot is gone, we must keep her off them until the baby comes and guard against another clot. Total bed rest. Once we get the baby out of there, she'll be fine, but I'd advise against any more."

After her discharge, Joe carried Candy upstairs, and she didn't come down for several weeks. Rod and Ricardo loaded the double bed from the guest room where Martha once stayed, and the older couple moved over to the carriage house for the remainder of the pregnancy. Martha tended to Candy, taking over the cooking, and watching after Eddie.

One evening when Candy and Martha were both upstairs, Rod asked Joe's advice—he still wanted to get Martha out of the dry cleaners, but she was adamant about keeping her job. Joe knew his mother needed to work, and she loved to sew. He talked to Conchesca, and they schemed to set Martha up in her own business: Martha's Mending and Tailoring.

While Rod and Martha remained at the carriage house, Juan and his crew converted her old bedroom into a sewing center. Juan drew up plans for shelves, cabinets, and a long cutting table. Christmas was approaching, and Rod got her a machine like the one she had at work—only better. Conchesca made up sample advertising fliers and created a logo. Martha had no idea what was going on with all the whispering, but it was Christmas, after all.

With Rodney Joseph's birth on December 6, Martha was too preoccupied to notice the secret conversations. Big brother was thrilled, and Eddie held baby Rod for hours. Candy supervised the decorating of the tree. Martha wondered when Rod didn't suggest they return home, but like every grandmother, she was thrilled to be around the new baby, and Candy still needed to keep her legs up. When he suggested they stay until Christmas Day, she agreed.

They had Christmas at Carlos's. Rod sat beside his mother at the table, with the sad realization that she probably wouldn't be with them the next year. Carlos blessed the food, and the old lady rapped her knuckles on the table.

"I have many blessings—all my children are healthy and prosperous and more great-grandchildren, but I want to say to you, Marta, God blessed the day He brought you and your family into Mario's life. That's all." She picked up her fork with a shaky hand.

Martha knelt beside her chair, leaning her head against her. "Gracias, Abuela."

The old lady patted her. "You have brought much happiness."

After dinner, Martha was puzzled when the entire family insisted on taking dessert to her house and leaving the weary grandmother with her nurse.

As much as she'd enjoyed being with the family, and appreciated that Mario had agreed to be with her at the Carriage House for Candy, she was looking forward to being home alone—and now everyone was descending on her house. She sighed.

Rod glanced over. "What, mi amor?"

"I love our family, but why does everyone want to traipse over here for dessert? And to take that poor baby out into this cold!"

He chuckled. "Patience. Maybe we have a Christmas surprise, no?" He took her hand and brought it to her lips. "Mamá was right, Marta. You have blessed this family—me most of all."

"I love you, Mario."

"She loves that you call me Mario."

"Why are you so slow? I want to be home!"

"Eager to get back to our big bed, are we, Marta?" Martha blushed. He loved to make his fair wife blush, and he laughed heartily as he pulled into their driveway. Cars and trucks were parked all down the street, but all the family had disappeared inside.

When they walked into the house, Candy was bouncing. She and Mérida stood together, hands linked and eyes sparkling. Conchesca and Jacinta were putting plates on the table, but looked up, smiling, and stopped. Linda set the cake down and took her doctor husband's hand.

Martha looked around for Joe. "We have a surprise for you, Mom." He led her upstairs. Beside the gleaming new sewing machine lay the draft brochures, and a large banner hung on the wall with the logo of her new business.

"Before you say anything, Martha, these are drafts," Conchesca hastened to tell her. "Make all the changes you want, and our accountant will run all the business end—your billing, taxes, Social Security—all you need to do is create your beautiful work and sew to your heart's content."

Martha walked over to Rod, who folded her in his arms. "My dream come true," she whispered. "How did you know?"

"You like it?" He led her to the machine. "If you want another, we can exchange it."

"This is too nice. How much did you pay for this, Mario?"

Everyone laughed, and Conchesca hugged her. "It's a write-off, Martha."

"You need the best equipment, mi amor, to make the finest things," Rod said.

Martha wandered around the room, lovingly rolling out the large drawers, running her hands along the long, smooth cutting table, and opening the cabinets to admire the shelves.

Over dessert and coffee, Conchesca reviewed the brochures with her, deciding on placement, and drawing up the price list. Martha loved the logo: an Appalachian woman sewing a quilt in her lap.

"Where is my chest?" she asked.

"We put it in the green bedroom," Juan said.

She rushed out, and they heard the squeak of the old wooden lid. She returned with a quilt in her hands. "Could we hang this?" she asked. All the women held it tenderly, admiring the tiny hand stitches. She told them the story of her "Freedom Quilt," first teaching them about the quilts secretly made by the slaves to map the way to the Underground Railroad.

"I started this quilt when I was seven years old—you see the childish stitches?" She pointed. "Every day after school I stayed in town until the library closed, and I walked to my house. This is my route: see the creek, and the bridge, the road down the hollow, and the big tree?"

"How long a walk was it Martha?" Linda asked.

"Four miles," Joe said. "When I was a kid, I walked to the hospital where Mom worked after school, and then over to the library until she came for me. We walked home every night. See the seasons?" She pointed to the spring, summer, fall, and winter quarters of the quilt pattern.

"Four miles!" The women exclaimed.

"That's why I don't mind to walk, Mario. This quilt is the only beauty that came out of those years."

Rod spread the quilt over the table, running his hands softly over it in awe. "How like you, mi amor, to make beauty from pain." Softly the clapping began. No one knew who started it.

"Abuela is right, Martha. You have brought much blessing to this family," Mérida whispered, and Jacinta agreed.

Martha looked around at all of them, spreading her arms. "You, all of you, you have taught us the meaning of family. Me, Joe, and Candy—you have given us a family."

Joe and Candy stood beside her. "We're grateful to all of you. Rod has been the only father Candy and I have ever known. Carlos gave us a home. Juan gave me a job, taught me how to drive, and helped me get my license..."

"And I'm going to give you a swirly, if you don't quit all this mush," Ricardo said, and Tomás volunteered to help. "But first, let's have more cake!" The Rodriguez men: overgrown boys.

Rod took Martha's hand. "What is this 'swirly' thing?"

Candy put her arm around his waist and explained the American high school prank of stuffing someone's head in the toilet and flushing it.

"But that is bullying!"

"Yes, Rod, it's bullying." Candy said.

He turned to Jacinta. "If this happens in your school, you call me at the station."

"Yes, Papá."

After all the laughter faded down the walkways and Rod and Martha were alone, he apologized for his boisterous family. She went around quietly blowing out candles and snapping off lamps. "Let's go upstairs, to our big bed."

He woke up at 4:25 and went to the bathroom. When he returned, he leaned against the headboard. He wanted to touch her thin, delicate hair, like spun glass. After the thick dark hair of his family, it remained a wonder to him, as were her light grey eyes. They were like the mist of the Appalachian Mountains in her native Kentucky. His hand hovered over her.

"I told you I don't fight, Mario."

She surprised him. He didn't know she was awake. "Why do you wear your hair short, Marta?"

"Don't go there. It was a weapon I removed—and I was beaten for it."

His hand dropped to finger her hair and then curve around her cheek. "Remember the night you whispered you wanted me to be safe? I dared to hope you loved me a little bit."

"Sometimes you talk too much," she said, tugging him down beside her.

That morning Rod decided they couldn't possibly make any more progress. He smiled as he dropped a kiss on his wife's cheek and crawled out of bed. She moved around the bedroom getting dressed. She was still shy, he thought, as he reached for his uniform pants. Remembering he'd spilled on them the day before, he grunted and jerked his belt out of the loops. It came out with a loud snap in the room.

Martha moved a step backward, watching him with round eyes.

"What?" he asked. But he immediately knew, and he dropped his belt on the floor, tossing his pants on a chair. "Marta," he whispered softly. "I spilled on my uniform, and I have to take to the cleaners." He held his arms out to her. "Will you come to me?"

She moved closer, and they met in the middle of the room.

"I love you, Marta." He took her into his arms.

She wept, and he kissed her tears as he held her

"Oh, My Love. I ask God to take away these fears, these memories. I will never hurt you."

She drew a deep breath and laid her long slender fingers on his chest. "I'm sorry."

"I'm sorry you were frightened. I didn't mean to frighten you."

"I know." She raised her face for his gentle kiss.

"We'll both be late—but I will make it up to you tonight." Rod brought his hand to her face, wiping away the tear that that slid down her cheek.

"I can't believe…"

"Believe it. God gave you to me."

"God gave me you, Mario."

Conlos Corners

In a month, Abuela left them quietly in her sleep. They laid her to rest beside her husband.

Martha had given her notice at work, and began stocking her shelves with fabrics and her drawers with thread and patterns. Juan carefully hung the quilt on the large wall behind her cutting table. She chose slat shutters for the big windows, and Joe installed recessed flood lighting throughout the room. They began advertising, and soon she had more work than she needed. As Rod had predicted, her business prospered. She made more money than she'd ever made in her life, and kept contributing to her Social Security.

The doctors still didn't want Candy working full time, but she missed her work. She loved to make people feel good, and she, too, was gifted to create beauty of a different kind. She contented herself doing manicures, but she wanted to do hair. Joe tried to help her be patient, reminding her how being home with Eddie after her vascular surgery was a blessing, and now she could enjoy little Rod's infancy. Rod Long—Joe was proud to name his son after his step-father.

Carlos stopped by Juan's Construction late one afternoon, asking his brother and Joe if they had a few minutes to come look at something. They drove over to a shopping plaza under development.

"What do you think, guys? We could fill this place. Conchesca and I can have a larger office suite in the center building. We could house your construction company in one of the spaces—probably two—and an electric company for Joe in another." They walked up and down the plaza. "We can rent the spaces we don't occupy, but look at this long narrow space, Joe. Couldn't we fix this up for Candy to have her own shop?"

The more the men talked, the more excited they got. "Conchesca can network all the businesses in the family. We'll have accounting do all the taxes, billing, and payroll—that would take a ton of work off your backs. We could even forward the phone calls to our secretary if you're out of the office. Our office space would be less than we are paying now."

"How much per square foot?" Juan asked.

Carlos had the data on going rates, and Juan said, "Without a middleman, I'd save money, too." He told Joe what he paid. "It's a good deal, Joe."

"You guys are ahead of me. I'm not in a position to buy inventory. Candy and I are debt free. We even bought our beater car with cash money, but you're talking about two start-ups, guys. I'm out. I'll keep working for you, Juan, but I'd like to get Candy out of that mall shop."

Juan and Carlos nodded, but later they drew up some proposals. Carlos bought the property and began looking for tenants. He said he'd fix up the beauty shop, leasing it to Candy after the business was up and going—no rent until she was pulling in salary. Joe agreed to let her look. She was thrilled, and happily spent her time off with her baby choosing the décor and fixtures. The doctors would allow her to work half-time by the time the shop would be ready, and one of the girls where she worked wanted to rent a station. When Conchesca told her she could wrap them into their benefit package, health insurance and paid vacation, another girl asked if she could come, too.

Juan took over completing construction, cutting their costs. They moved his company over to the new location. Carlos put up signs announcing the opening of Conlos Corners and listing the establishments. Beside Candy's Cuts and Curls was a jeweler, an older man and his wife. Juan would be on the other side of Carlos's huge complex, now housing his tech company and Mérida's graphic design and printing. Carlos and Juan ignored Joe's questions about the next location, but they advertised for the large building on the far end, and a carpet/flooring dealer wanted to look at the space one evening. Carlos was waiting for him to show up.

Jacinta's Second Chance

John Gilbert pulled into Conlos Corners when Jacinta stopped by after school. He noticed her getting out of her car, raising her arms to pull pins out of the bun that captured her luxurious raven curls at the base of her neck. Oblivious to his stares, she shook her locks free, and they spilled over her shoulders. John held his breath and followed behind her as she walked into Carlos Internet Consultants. He introduced himself to Carlos, and they shook hands while Carlos's hand circled the beauty's waist, and he pulled her in for a peck on the cheek. "Jacinta Rodriguez, Mr. John Gilbert."

John thought it was an innocent peck for his wife, but he checked her hand and noticed she didn't wear a ring.

Instantly, Jacinta's warm dark brown eyes turned into black ice. "John Gilbert? Would you happen to be the father of Elissa and Merry Gilbert?"

"Uh, yes, they're my daughters, Ms. Rodriguez," John said, wondering why that name seemed so familiar.

She crossed her arms and glared at him. "I have left half a dozen messages for you, Mr. Gilbert! Do you not care about your girls' education? I'm trying to schedule an IEP, and since we have no Mrs. Gilbert, I'm stuck trying to chase you down while you ignore my calls."

"Ms. Rodriguez, I assure you I care about my daughters' education. I've been meaning to call you, but..."

Conchesca rounded the corner. "Carlos, Honey, the gentleman on the phone insists he must talk with you. Can you excuse us for a moment, Sir?"

John could have sworn he saw Carlos pat the newcomer on her backside before he quickly flipped a set of keys to the indomitable Ms. Rodriguez.

"Sis, come down off your high horse and help me out here. I'm trying to run a business. Show him the space on the far end. I'll be there as soon as I can."

Tossing those magnificent tresses over her shoulder, Jacinta marched ahead of Mr. Gilbert. Two girls, first and third graders from her school, cried out the window of a van with the name *Gilbert's Floor Coverings* emblazoned on the side. Her eyes lit up and she walked quickly to the vehicle, stepping on the running board to talk to the children. Her pencil skirt clung to her fabulous backside, and John knew he was in big trouble.

"I like your hair down, Ms. Rodriguez."

John mentally agreed with his older daughter, and an image of running his hands though those thick curls popped into his befuddled brain.

His girls babbled enthusiastically. This was *the* Ms. Rodriguez, the most fabulous and beloved teacher in the school. He felt like running his head into the brick wall as he stood, waiting. She had no problem with his girls. She laughed, running her fingers through their hair, and asked if they had their homework.

"Oh, Daddy always does homework with us. We go to the shop, and he helps us. Don't you, Daddy?" Elissa asked.

"Why are we here?" Merry wanted to know.

"I have to look at some property, Sweetie," John said. "We'll go for an ice cream in a few minutes Can you be patient a bit longer, girls?"

Jacinta backed off the step, and he caught her arm as she tottered on high heels only a Latina woman could pull off. "The space is vacant," she said. "It wouldn't hurt to let them come along,"

"Can we, Daddy?" the girls begged.

He opened the van door. Elissa hopped down and Merry reached out her arms for him. He swung her up into his arms, but she suddenly realized her sister was holding the teacher's hand. She wiggled down and ran to catch them, grabbing the Jacinta's other hand. John, bereft of his girls, followed morosely, but she dropped the girls' hands to pull the keys out of her pocket and jiggle them into the lock.

Merry looked for her father to pick her up; that was better. When Jacinta looked back, he was snuggling the little girl's neck and making her giggle.

"I love you, Daddy. I missed you all day. I made a one hundred on my letters. Wanna see?"

"I do. But, by this time I'm not surprised. You did them perfectly last night. How did your spelling test go, Elissa?"

She frowned, "I missed that stupid e after the c, but I got all the rest of them."

"That's a ninety-five! We'll get it next time, okay?"

"Okay, Daddy. What's this?"

"Daddy's looking for new space for his business, girls, so I have to talk grown-up talk now. Stay close by."

Jacinta watched him with new regard. "Here, girls." When fishing for the keys, Jacinta felt a piece of chalk in her pocket. She leaned over quickly, drawing a hop-scotch grid on the concrete floor and threw them the chalk for a marker.

John stove manfully to keep his eyes from being glued to that female backside, with the curves in all the right places. What was happening to him? He hadn't looked at a woman in over six years. Dating was impossible for a single father.

When they began playing, Jacinta walked him across the space. At the far end, she asked, "Where's their mother?"

"She was furious when I didn't agree to an abortion, but I bribed her to carry Merry, promising her a pretty nice sum. As soon as she was born, her mother left with a boyfriend, and we haven't heard anything from her since."

"She hasn't seen her own daughters?" Jacinta whispered, her eloquent eyes wide.

"Nope. I'd just as soon she didn't. I won full custody in an uncontested divorce. She wanted Merry dead, and she never was a good mother to Elissa. I was a fool to let it happen the second time, but I wouldn't give anything for that precious girl now. She is well named."

"Why did you chose that name?"

"She was born on Christmas Day. Her mother left her in the nursery and checked out of the hospital, never looking back."

Jacinta touched his arm. "I'm sorry." He shrugged. "You were left with a baby and a three-year-old. How did you manage?"

"Elissa went to preschool, and I had a crib and a playpen in the shop. I carried Merry around in a front pack the first six months, and a back pack until she was walking, which was probably delayed because I had her in the backpack so much."

Obviously wanting to change the subject, he asked her questions about the building, and she consulted the sheet her brother had shoved in her hand. She quoted him the price per square foot for rent and for purchase.

"It's a fair price—better than I pay now, but I'd have moving costs. I have a lot of inventory. I wasn't planning to move, but this is a terrific location, and I wanted to see it."

"Moving wouldn't be a problem," Jacinta assured him. "You don't know my brothers."

He looked at her skeptically. "How many brothers do you have?"

"Four: Carlos, Tomás, Ricardo, and Juan, then add Joe, my brother-in-law, and they'd swarm the place and get you moved. Joe Long is one of us. They'd get it done."

John stepped off the space, looked at the floor plan again, and commented he'd need a wall to separate the showroom from storage in the back. "Didn't the ad say they'd build to suit?"

"Yes, Juan's construction company is coming into the space next to Carlos's computer business. That would be a good match for you. When he builds a house, he can refer you customers. How much showroom space do you need, and how much storage?" When he estimated, she asked if the storage area needed improvements.

"Not much. 'As is' would be fine, as long as it's weatherproof. Concrete floors in the storage area is okay, but I need a nice showroom in front."

"Hmm." The pencil tapped on her full red lips. "In that case, we can reduce the price and give you a cut on the storage area."

"Don't you think you need to ask your brother?" John kept glancing over to check on his daughters, smiling fondly.

"Mr. Gilbert, I am Carlos's little sister. He rarely refuses me. I don't know if he's *ever* refused me, come to think of it."

"Call me John," he said, with a twinkle in his eye. He doubted he could refuse her anything, either, if she looked at him with those luminous dark eyes.

"Jacinta; sometimes my brothers shorten it to 'Cinta, but it's spelled with a J. Papá can't surround a J. He pronounces it 'y,' the Spanish way for foreign words. My stepmother is Martha, and he calls her 'Marta.' It's so cute."

"Sounds like an amazing family."

"I'm blessed. Now, while I have your attention, may I talk to you about the girls?"

He walked toward his daughters, but she held him back. He looked down at the long, perfectly manicured fingers resting on his arm. Fire engine red. He wondered if her toenails matched.

"I'm really sorry I didn't return your calls. Every day I try to get my running around done, my estimates made up, and my orders called in before the girls get off the bus. It drops them off at the shop. Then we have homework, home to fix dinner, baths, story time, and another day is done." He shrugged. "Except, once they are down, I do billing."

"I don't know how you do it."

"I wonder myself. What do you need?"

"Do you know what an IEP is?" She explained the Individual Education Plan, and told him the school was recommending they be tested for gifted. "I'm Elissa's teacher, and I have no doubt she's a gifted student. Merry's teacher feels the same. Do you object?"

John grilled her, asking perceptive questions about what that would mean for his girls educationally and socially, and finally said he'd pray about it. He promised to call her in two days.

John Gilbert took the space the next evening and asked where she was when he came to sign the paperwork.

"She's tied up in meetings this afternoon," Carlos said. "Did you need to ask her something? Do you need her number?"

"She gave it to me. I told her I'd make a decision about the girls. I'll call her tonight."

He did, after the girls were in bed, and they talked a long time. She agreed to bring Merry's teacher by Conlos Corners Friday afternoon, since the shopping center was near her home. While they were in the conference room, Mérida showed the girls her printing shop, and put them in front of the computers with an art program while the teachers explained what would be involved in testing John's children.

Carlos rounded the corner to pour two cups of coffee for himself and his wife. "Gilbert, what are you doing here? Juan, my brother and construction manager, will start on your specs next week, and it won't take long. Joe Long, our electrician and HVAC guy, will run a duct into the storage area, and we'll have the wall set by the end of the week. I'm sure you want to wall off the commode and sink as well. It's all right in the back? When you have a minute, come look at the drawings."

After the teacher conference, Carlos and John discussed his space. They shook hands when they finished their discussion, and Carlos invited him to his house for a barbecue. "Bring your girls. We've heard all about them. 'Cinta loves them. We'll have tons of kids in the yard; it's a kid's birthday party. Whose party, Sis?"

Jacinta rolled her expressive eyes. "Your niece."

"That narrows it down to about five."

"Maribella, doting uncle." Jacinta told John the birthday girl would be six, close to Merry's age, and when he said he'd ask them, she walked him to Mérida's office. After learning Ms. Rodriguez would be there, the girls were excited to go.

"We're done here, Munchkins. Ready for ice cream and cake?"

"Wanna ride with us, Ms. Rodriguez?" Merry slipped her little hand into Jacinta's.

John held his breath. Between her family and his, maybe they could progress his wannabe relationship.

"Merry, we can't put your daddy on the spot like that. Maybe someone is joining you."

"You mean, like a date?" Elissa asked. "Daddy never dates. Mrs. Gooding says he's a hermit."

John ran his fingers through his blond hair and shook his head.

Jacinta already had him pegged as a good-looking guy. He was tall, blond, and had brilliant blue eyes that had the habit of searching her face for clues, like he was doing now.

In his deep voice, John added to the invitation. "You're most welcome."

"I'll lead you in my car. They'll be tired afterward, and you'll need to get them home to bed."

Mérida busied herself closing down her computer, but she was holding back a grin.

And that's how the relationship progressed. Afternoon meetings, ice cream treats, and birthday parties. Most afternoons, Jacinta dropped the girls at John's shop after school. In the Rodriguez family, a birthday or anniversary occurred almost every week, and John became a fixture. Mérida warned her papá not to push it, and Martha helped her tone him down.

"It is past time for Jacinta to be married and making babies," Rod said.

One Saturday afternoon, Carlos's yard was filled with screaming, playing children, and Rod looked at his daughter sitting on a glider beside John. She pushed off, her red toenails flashing in her yellow sandals. John's younger daughter, Merry, sprawled on Jacinta's lap, her sweaty golden curls plastered against her cheek. Jacinta idly stroked her as she talked with John who laughed, putting his arm behind her and toying with her ponytail, twirling the curls around a finger.

"Do you think he's kissed her?"

"Mario Rodriguez, that is none of your business," Martha said, but she looked at him fondly. "Now hush that kind of talk."

"Make me," he teased, and she did, kissing him soundly.

"PDA, Papá," Tomás shouted. "Remember, we have little ones watching."

"The privilege of being married," Rod replied before he lowered his lips again.

The crowd shouted laughter, and Joe slipped his arm around Candy's waist. "We're married," he said, before he tasted her sweet lips.

"Rod wants to show us something later, after the party. Are you game?" Joe asked.

"What is it?"

"The elderly lady two doors down from them died. He caught her daughter talking to a realtor, and told her we might be interested. Saves both of us the listing fees."

Candy's sweet face puckered into a thoughtful frown. "The red brick?"

"I think that's it. He went inside, said it's not in bad shape. The carpets are worn and need replacing, and the linoleum is dated."

"Maybe John would go with us and take a look."

Joe glanced over at the couple. "Won't be long before we're having another wedding. I wonder what Papá thinks about blonde grandchildren."

"Eddie's blond." Candy had become accustomed to thinking of the Rodriguez family as their own, and Joe knew it.

"Yes, he is, and Rod is his abuelo, no?" Joe replied with a chuckle.

When the children were doing more squabbling than playing, the adults gathered them up and sorted them into various vans.

John took Merry out of Jacinta's arms and when he hoisted her to his shoulder, she woke and reached her arm down. Jacinta took her hand, bringing it to her lips to kiss it.

"Are we leaving, Daddy? I don't want to go."

"We are going to look at a house with Miss Candy and Mr. Joe."

She pointed to the carriage House. "That's their house."

"They might move," he explained. He took Elissa's hand and walked across the yard.

"Girls, tell Miss Conchesca thank you for the nice time."

"Thank you. We had a good time at the party, and the food was scrumptious. How do you say it?"

"Delicioso," Conchesca replied. "Thank you for coming—my nephew, Armando, likes you, I think. He pulled your braid, no? That's a sure sign."

Elissa blushed and ducked behind her father.

Candy and Joe joined the couple, explaining where the house was, and they took the lead because John's car seats were in the big commercial van, and baby Rod's car seat was in their car.

They walked through the house, which was smaller than Rod and Martha's. But they wouldn't have more children, so three bedrooms were plenty, especially with an office for Joe downstairs.

John did a quick estimate in his head, guessing at the square footage, and trailed behind the family.

Rod was talking to the heir in the front yard, and she walked in with him, pointing out various nice things about the house and honestly noting the necessary repairs.

"The agent wants me to make considerable repairs before I list it," she told them, "but Officer Rodriguez tells me you can do them. That would be such a relief. I need to get back to my job in D.C."

Joe didn't know the first thing about buying a house, but Rod told the lady if the kids liked it, they'd go to the bank the next day and get back with her in the afternoon.

Eddie's grey eyes danced. Joe loved this quiet boy, and drew him close. "What do you think, son? Do you like this house?"

"Can we move here? I could see mis abuelos every day!"

"The bus stops right across the street, Eddie," Rod told him.

Eddie tugged on his mother's hand. Let's go upstairs. I want to see my bedroom."

"Don't get ahead of yourself. Daddy has to see if he can afford this."

Eddie sobered immediately. "Yes, Sir." But he ran up the steps. "This would be my room—if we buy it," he said. "I can see your sewing room from here." The boy looked at Martha, and she placed her hand on his shoulder, looking out the window.

"We can't use tin can phones, but maybe we can rig up some signal flags."

"Don't get his hopes up, Mom."

John admired this family, and watched Martha put her arm around Rod's waist and linger behind as the Long family moved down the hall to the master bedroom.

"John, I remember a time when I longed for Marta to reach for me." Rod winked. "My mamá said, 'God blessed the day He sent Marta to our family.' Remember, Marta? It was Christmas, before she died." Rod pulled her into his arms. "I can never give Him back what He has given me in you and your children."

"Mario, your family has been too good to us."

John already knew this was a remarkable family, but he listened to Rod's answer. "Mérida threw away money and her education until she became Candy's friend. She returned from that trip to Mississippi no longer a flighty little girl, but a sober and thoughtful young woman, counting her blessings. Joe has worked right alongside Juan, building his business. And you helped Jacinta..." Rod looked at John and stopped.

Thankfully, the cries to hurry moved them down the hall. Candy's eyes were shining. "Look out the window. What a beautiful yard! This is a huge room!" She spun around. "Missy will come over from West Virginia and help me."

Rod invited them all over to their house for tortilla soup. Eddie ran down the stairs whooping and beat them down the street. Martha whipped up some cornbread, and John's girls played a board game. They didn't know it, but Eddie explained it to them—he was patient and kind, like his father. The boy wanted to sleep in their new house, but Joe cautioned him once again not to count his chickens. After dessert, they left for home, and John and Jacinta left for his place.

Rod studied his daughter as they parted.

"Papá, I don't sleep there. My car is there. I'll go home." She hugged him.

"I've wanted to have a word with you, Sir," John said, "if you have a moment."

"Come in, then." Rod led the way back inside, winking at Martha. The men disappeared into his study, but soon came out.

"I'll love those girls like I love Eddie and Little Rod, but make me some more grandbabies, too, okay?" he said to his daughter.

"Mario, give the man a chance to propose in his own way," Martha fussed.

Rod waved his hand. "Okay, do it."

Jacinta buried her face in her hands.

John dropped on one knee in front of her. "With your papá's permission, Jacinta, will you do me the honor of becoming my wife?"

Elissa and Merry joined hands and danced in a circle, and then Merry threw her arms around Jacinta. "Can we call you Mommy now?"

"Girls, she must say yes," John cautioned.

"Say yes, 'Cinta. Marry us," Elissa begged. "Please?"

Jacinta drew the two giggling girls into her arms. "Yes, I will marry you." She looked up at John.

He was standing now, and he pulled a ring box out of his pocket. "This isn't exactly the romantic scene I envisioned, but I love you Jacinta, and I want to spend the rest of my life with you."

"Tomorrow, leave the girls with us and take her to a fabulous dinner," Rod suggested.

"I'll take you up on that, Sir."

"Now," Rod rubbed his hands together, "when's the wedding? You want a big wedding, small wedding?"

"Honestly, Mario! Go kids." Martha waved them out the door. They heard her gentle fussing as the door closed and then silence.

"Is he saying anything?" Elissa asked.

"I don't think Papá is talking, and neither is Martha. I know my papá."

"Ooooh, I get it," Elissa said, grinning and looking up at her father. "Now you must kiss Jacinta too, Daddy."

Chuckling, he brushed his lips against hers. "More on that later," he whispered.

Elissa stood back and crossed her arms. "Is that the best you can do?"

John grabbed her by the waist and ran to the van. "That is enough out of you!" But he was laughing, and Elissa knew she wasn't in trouble.

She crawled in the back seat. "Let me fasten your seat belt, Merry."

"I can do it!" the younger girl retorted.

"If you girls are good, I'll read you a story before I leave tonight," Jacinta promised. And she did. She toweled them dry after their bath, and read them a story, smelling their sweet strawberry shampoo as they leaned against her. She listened to their prayers, tucked them into bed, and kissed each forehead.

John watched from the door. Merry held up her hands, and he crossed the room to kiss them both. "'Night, Daddy. Is our mommy going to spend the night here?" Merry asked.

"Not tonight, Sweetie. You'll have to be our flower girl first."

"Soon?"

"If you don't let us discuss it, we'll be old and grey before the wedding."

Elissa giggled. "Go talk, Daddy. 'Night, Mommy."

John left the room shaking his head. "I hope you're good with this, Jacinta. Between your father and my girls, you didn't have much choice." At the foot of the stairs, he took her into his arms and gave her the kiss of pent-up longing he'd held all day. Hearing a giggle, he looked up to see the tails of two pink nightgowns disappearing into the girls' bedroom. "What are you girls doing out of bed!"

"That's *much* better, Daddy." Elissa and Merry giggled, and the couple heard the sound of the beds creaking ominously as they jumped into them.

Jacinta held her hand in front of her face, trying to hold the laughter back.

"I'm sorry," John began, but she interrupted him.

"I loved those girls before I met you, John."

"You don't mind a ready-made family?" He held her back and looked into those dancing black eyes. "I'll let them stay with someone in your family, and we'll have a honeymoon to ourselves, I promise."

"The family will fight over them. If we have a small wedding, we can have time to take a vacation with the girls before summer is over."

"We can't have a small wedding—inviting your family is a village."

"Now who's talking about a ready-made family? The Rodriguez family comes as a package deal."

"As an only child, alone when my parents died, I'm enjoying being a part of this great family."

"Our family brings everyone in. We can't imagine being without Martha, Joe and Candy."

John fixed some lemonade, and they sat on the deck. Jacinta told him the story of the Long family. "Eddie isn't his?"

"Don't let Joe hear you! He bristles if anyone even suggests that. Maybe someday you'll see the pictures of their wedding. Candy was big as a house, but he insisted he wanted to marry her before Eddie was born, because he wanted his name on the birth certificate. And he prayed to be like another Joseph, Mary's husband. He waited for her to have the baby."

"Amazing."

"He is amazing." She told him Candy's nightmare of abuse, and who Eddie's birth father was. "Mérida went with Candy when her mother was dying, and they went to the trailer where she lived. She came back and told Papá she'd been to hell. Candy and Martha were both horribly abused. Martha was beaten as a child and as a wife. I'll show you her freedom quilt. Papá and Joe taught them both to trust. God has been faithful."

"They seem to be loving wives now. I'd never guess they had issues."

Jacinta slapped her arm. "Mosquitos are out. I'm going inside. I need to go anyway."

"We didn't decide on a date."

"Sooner rather than later, or Papá will accuse me of being aged." She looked into his eyes, watching them darken with the passion he felt. "And John, I was raised in a loving home. Mamá and Papá had seven children—I have no issues. Don't wait!"

"Let's talk to the preacher tomorrow, then, and get it set up. I'm really glad you don't want to have an elaborate wedding that takes months to plan."

"I don't want to wait. I've waited a long time for you, and now that I've found you, I don't want to waste another minute."

"You'd better leave while I can still let you go." John kissed her cheek lightly, but she understood why.

"I'll be over for breakfast. I promised the girls I'd take them to day camp, and then I have to help this handsome guy set up his new stock." She stepped out on the front porch and blew him a kiss.

Jacinta's Wedding

Martha pushed the door to Candy's beauty shop open. She felt wonderment at her sense of belonging. She was the mother of the bride. Candy had hung the closed sign on the front door. The wedding party and her two fellow beauticians locked themselves inside and began preparing Martha and the bride's sisters. The sisters-in-law agreed to ride herd on the children. Elissa, Merry, and Candy's toddler were the only children in the wedding party. The other children were given roles as distributors of birdseed bags, cake servers, and other minor positions. Each would have a special corsage.

Candy was nose to nose with the bride. After six years, Candy had learned to hold her own with the Latino passion in the Rodriguez family. Candy wanted Jacinta's hair down, the way John liked it, but Jacinta insisted on having it up, with tendrils curling down the side of her face.

"I have a tiara to hold my veil. I need the hair out of my way."

Finally, heaving a huge sigh, Candy agreed. "Have it your way, but before you leave for the trip, I will brush it out."

"Deal," Jacinta said, with a note of triumph.

"Sit," Candy ordered. "Mom, are you good?"

Martha had watched the entire battle, amused by her daughter-in-law holding her own with the strong-willed woman. She remembered the timid, frightened little teenager her son had married, and silently blessed her husband and his wonderful family. At his request, her silver hair now fell to her shoulders. It was a little thing she could give him, after he had taught her to love and trust and given her the first family she'd ever known. In fact, she was rewarded every time he softly touched her fine hair and she saw the wonder in his eyes.

"I'm good, Sweetie. Not much you can do with an old lady's hair."

Nancy, the beautician who had started in the shop when it opened, disagreed. "Your hair is lovely, and we will make Officer Rod look at you with longing."

Everyone joined the laughter after Jacinta commented her father always looked at Martha with longing. "You light up Papá's life, Martha. And I appreciate it that you keep him from interfering with ours."

"Papá will always interfere with us, 'Cinta," Mérida said, "but he has settled down a lot."

"He will be happy when all of his children are married," Martha said. "He has great respect for the institution of marriage."

"Yeah—he walks around with a perpetual smile now that he has you in his bed."

Martha was used to this rowdy family and the intimacy among them, but once in a while, they still threw her for a loop.

Candy gave her a quick pat on the shoulder, and she relaxed. "I was scared to death to get married, but my counselors told me God made them two by two and man was not made to live alone. And now we need to embarrass the bride! Who gave her the fire-engine red teddy? Mer? Wasn't it you?"

"Yep! Works for me," Mérida said, "but the slinky black thing Conchesca gave her won the prize."

A light tap sounded at the door, and Candy peeped through the closed blinds. "It's Carlos, button up the girl talk." She opened the door, but only wide enough for him to hand in a tray with flutes of mimosas, which he restricted to the wedding party, cautioning the hairdressers to abstain until the haircuts were completed.

Candy and Martha, victims of alcohol-fueled abusers, never touched the stuff, but they were tolerant when others indulged moderately. Candy handed Nancy a bottle of volumizer, suggesting she use a bit of the new product on Martha's hair.

Jacinta's thick mane, on the other hand, had to be tamed, and Candy combed her long locks with a different product, complaining, "This is a sin, 'Cinta, to take your luscious curls out."

"No one is ever satisfied with her hair," Nancy said. "Those with curls want it straight and those with straight want a perm."

"Yours is perfect, Candy. With those soft curls and your big, dark grey eyes, you are a real beauty," Mérida said, giving her an affectionate hug.

Candy appeared surprised and shook her head. *Work never seemed this much fun*, she thought, with her wonderful family surrounding her, jokes and teasing flying back and forth. The bride didn't want to leave, and sat around while the rest of the wedding party got dolled up.

Finally, Conchesca invited them all to their offices, where they had set up sandwiches, and the party moved next door.

Martha promised to help with the girls, and Candy sent a text to the groom, telling him she was ready for his daughters. He brought them into the beauty shop, and she told him Jacinta insisted she'd wear her hair up, but she made her promise to let it down it when they left for their trip. The girls planned to stay with their Aunt Mérida, who now lived in the Carriage House, while John and Jacinta had a few days to themselves. She cautioned the girls not to play hard until after the wedding, and sent them on their way. Heaving a sigh, she sat on a chair by the desk and rested her head on her arms.

Martha let Joe into the shop, and he immediately walked over to massage his wife's shoulders. "How's the leg?"

Candy leaned back into his chest. "Okay. I wore my surgical stockings."

"Everyone looks gorgeous. You look lovely, Mom. I brought you both some lunch." Joe went to the back and brewed some tea for her.

She went to the chairs in the waiting area and put her feet up. She reached for the sandwiches. "Tell me about the lamp discovery, Joe."

Giving a self-deprecating laugh, Joe shrugged. "I saw this huge lot of ceiling lights going for almost nothing, so I ordered one to see if they could be repaired. It was a nothing fix, a couple of crossed wires straightened out, and I can sell them for full price. Juan ordered the whole lot. I've taught Carlos's boy how to do it, and we'll make a ton of money. Carlos wants me to open my own place in the empty spot past the construction company. I planned to keep working for Juan. What do you think?"

As she munched, she asked questions, and they prayed. With a bit of a loan from Carlos, they could purchase inventory.

"I don't want you to walk today. You've been on your feet enough. Do we have time to go home?"

"The wedding is at four—thank God the weather has cooperated."

"Why don't you rest at Mérida's? Didn't you bring your dress?"

"Where are the boys?"

"The nanny's watching them run with the cousins."

"I hope they don't tear up the yard! Let's go." Candy went to the back and got her dress and shoes. Joe brought the car down in front of her shop and helped her in.

When they pulled into to the carriage house, Mérida walked out and helped carry Candy's things inside. "Come into your old home. How are you doing?" No one knew Candy better than her best friend. Mérida looked closely at her. "Come inside and lie down until time to go. The boys are fine; Little Rod's asleep in the big house."

Candy followed her inside. Within minutes, she was sleeping in the downstairs bedroom.

Joe tiptoed in about 3:15 and sat on the edge of the bed. She opened her eyes and lifted her arms. Gathering her in an embrace, he kissed her. "I hate to wake you, but Mérida said you needed time to prepare."

"I do." Candy started to swing her legs off the bed, but Joe caught her feet and rubbed them. "That feels good—but you're checking for swelling, aren't you?"

He patted her calves and grinned. "Not too bad. Do you still want to walk?"

"I need to corral Rod. I hope he doesn't put the ring in his mouth."

Joe chuckled. "Mom sewed it on the pillow. Carlos has snips to cut it loose at the altar." He leaned to brush his lips on her forehead. "I'll get the boys dressed. See you in a few."

Mérida and Candy circled the house to avoid the guests. Joe had done an excellent job with the boys. Rod looked adorable in his little tux, and Eddie was satisfied in a suit to match his daddy.

"You look pretty, Mommy," the older boy said.

"And don't my men look handsome!" she replied.

Conchesca called everyone into the family room, where the processional would form into a line. John's girls were handed their baskets of flower petals, and the two little ones stepped out of the house when the music began.

Joe and Eddie had taken Martha down the aisle, and they sat with her. They turned to watch the processional. All the bridesmaids and the ring bearer came forward, Candy walking immediately in front of little Rod, who was clutching the pillow. She beckoned him to follow, and he walked, wandering from left to right, smiling up at folks, and heading for his daddy the moment he saw him. Candy gently took his hand and pointed him to the front. He thrust the pillow into Carlos's hands and ran back to Joe, to the amusement of all the guests. Joe settled him in his lap and snuggled him, whispering that he'd done a fine job.

Papá Rod proudly bore his daughter to her waiting groom, putting her hand in his with a smile and returning to sit beside Martha, taking her hand in his own. Overwhelmed with gratitude, he patted it, and she smiled.

After the ceremony, Joe insisted Candy sit, and he brought a footrest. She rolled her eyes, but reveled in his loving concern. After he brought her a plate of food and a drink, he tried to get young Rod off her lap, but the toddler had missed his mother and refused to move.

"He's fine, Joe." Little Rod leaned on her breast, rubbing it softly with his pudgy hands. Tomás came by and then Ricardo, wanting to know if she needed anything. Juan wanted to dance with her, but Joe said she needed to be off her feet. He pulled up a chair and looked around the yard. He chuckled at the Rodriguez brothers clowning among themselves.

"What a great family," he said. "They've been mighty good to us."

"For a couple of only children, we've scored big time, haven't we?" Candy replied. "Mérida is the best friend I've ever had. She's like a sister."

"Remember when I said Rod had been good for Mom? They all said how good she was for him. She's not the same woman."

"She is, Joe. She's loyal and loving, stable and hard-working, always doing for others—but she's happy."

"Yeah, you're right. And you are strong and capable—not the timid little girl I married."

"You don't seem to mind."

Curving his hand around her neck, Joe claimed a kiss. "I like my strong, capable woman!" He grinned and leaned closer. "And I can't wait to get you home, all to myself."

"Ah, now I know why you insisted on a nap!" Candy ran a finger over his lips.

He took a deep breath. "You ready to go now?"

They laughed, and touched their foreheads together.

"Look at our kids," Rod said, nodding toward the couple. He laced his fingers with Martha's. "They've come a long way."

"So have we, Mario. You and your family have brought us healing and wholeness."

"You don't know what you have done for me. You are my north star. Your gentle courage has been an inspiration for my children. They are no longer lost in foolishness or materialism. We needed you, Marta. Mamá knew that."

She leaned her head on his shoulder as his arm circled her waist. To be with a man and be safe was a wonder to her, and tears stung her eyes. She brought her hand to his chest, and he captured it.

A burst of laughter drew their attention to the newlyweds, who were approaching their departure time. John was obviously eager to depart.

Candy stood to capture the bride's hand. "Come on. I get my way now." She led Jacinta into the house to carefully brush out her luxurious hair. "I promised John when he brought the girls in. Didn't they look cute?"

"Precious. I'll miss them."

"We'll take care of them. You concentrate on that handsome man of yours!"

"Looking forward to that. Which should I try first, the red teddy or the black gown?"

"Neither one will be on too long!" Candy giggled and hugged her. She helped her pop on a green sundress. "Go, have fun."

Jacinta stepped into the inevitable pair of slinky stilettos.

"I don't know how you can walk in those things."

"It's an art form," Jacinta said. Shaking out her glorious black curls, she rose and walked toward her groom, waiting in the gazebo.

As Candy knew he would, he tangled his hands in her hair and drew her into a lingering kiss. She allowed them a moment of privacy before carrying out the tray of birdseed bags and gathering the nieces together for the distribution.

Laughing, John Gilbert linked hands with the new Mrs. Gilbert, and they ran to their waiting car—gaily decorated by the Rodriguez men. They were off as cameras flashed. Carlos and Conchesca, the first to marry, had to dodge following cars and escape honking pursuers. This night, every couple was happily married, and looked forward to their own privacy. Only the baby, Mérida, remained single. Women caught up in the romance of the wedding, and men sharing the longing of the groom, broke away quickly to head for their own homes. Carlos brushed them all aside—a crew would come in the morning to clean up.

Rod looked at Martha—Mérida was right, he always looked at her with longing—but now she saw the passion in his soft brown eyes and took his hand with a smile. "Come home, mi amor," he whispered. He saw her little tremor of pleasure and winked.

Joe chased down his boys. Looping an arm around little Rod, he hung him under one arm like a sack of potatoes and grabbed Eddie's hand, steering his family to the truck. Candy patted him on the butt before putting a thumb through his belt loop and leaning against him. Yes, he was proud of his strong, confident woman.

Mérida's Forbidden Love

Candy was startled when she heard the door rattle. The shade was drawn; the shop was closed, but she worked on the books after hours. Joe had a key. Who could it be? She pulled she shade to the side and saw Mérida, so she opened the door.

"What's up, Girl?"

"Do you have a moment? I have a problem."

"Sure, what is it?"

"This guy answered my ad for help. He's well trained, and very gifted—perfect for the job—but I have a problem." Candy waited. "He's illegal."

"Oh, dear! Your daddy hates illegals, and he's a cop."

"You're not telling me anything I don't know. But, the worst part of it is...I like him, Candy. I mean...you know."

"I thought you'd sworn off men since Sam ran around on you."

"He found someone who'd give him what he wanted, and I'm glad I found out before I married the jerk. Francisco is Mexican. He's dignified, aristocratic-looking, tall, slender, and handsome. He's been to the finest schools in his country, and he knows his stuff."

"What did you say to him?"

"I told him to come back Friday after I've interviewed others. But I need him; he's perfect for the job."

"If he's illegal, how can you pay him? He'd have no social security, no benefits. That's not right. Besides, you'd never keep it from Rod. He knows everything." Joe pushed open the door and took in the women's concern in a glance. He pulled a chair next to Candy and asked what was up, and Mérida told him her problem.

"From what you say about his education and background, it sounds like a story there somewhere. Is Carlos still here? Let's talk to him," Joe suggested.

"Carlos will never hire an illegal," Mérida said. "The Rodriguez family never hires an illegal."

"Why is he illegal? Can we help him out?"

"I don't know, but he seems like an upright guy. He said he entered the country legally, but he's over-stayed his visa for some reason."

"Carlos is reasonable guy, and he might be able to help him out. He knows a lot of people."

They locked up and returned to the center office, where Carlos was closing up for the night. He paused, looking up when he saw Mérida enter with Joe and Candy.

"What?"

Mérida blinked back tears, and turned to Candy, who briefly relayed the information.

Carlos wouldn't have taken his sister seriously a couple of years ago, but her friendship with Candy had matured her. She'd dumped the two-timer, finished her degree, and built a good little business for herself. Now she needed help. She handed him her applicant's portfolio. He glanced over it, raising his eyebrows at the educational background and obvious skills he brought to the position.

"Why would a guy like this be illegal?"

"I don't know. He said he over-stayed his visa," Mérida said.

Carlos blew out a long breath. "Is this his phone number? Can we call him?" She nodded. "Let's ask him if he can come back and bring his passport and visa with him."

Carlos picked up the phone and dialed the number. "Mr. Vargas, this is Carlos Rodriguez, Mérida Rodriguez's oldest brother. She has brought your information to me, and we have some questions about your...er...status. Would you be willing to discuss it more fully with us? I see. Would you mind bringing your passport and visa? Give me the address where you're staying, and I'll swing by. I'll take you home to dinner then."

"Mérida, I can't promise you anything, but he doesn't sound like someone who is illegal for no reason. He is staying with a prominent Hispanic family. Let's pick him up and go home. I'll call Conchesca and tell her to set two more places for dinner."

Candy and Joe left to pick up their boys at Martha and Rod's after school. Young Rod was in preschool now, and Eddie was in third grade. Candy touched Mérida's hand briefly before they parted and gave it a squeeze. "We'll pray," she whispered.

With two rowdy boys, the Longs didn't have much time to pray. Shortly after the boys were down, Mérida called. Tucking her legs under her, Candy listened to the story. Francisco brought his mother up to Houston for cancer treatments, which proved unsuccessful, but on their way out of Mexico, at the Brownsville crossing, they were eye-witnesses to the drug-related murder of a U.S. border guard. The cartel runners chased them across the border, firing at them. They thought they'd escaped, but apparently, the bad guys traced their tags and had been sending threats via phone. When Vargas changed his phone, they got notes delivered to their hotel. When his mother died, he sent her body home and fled to a distant cousin living in Columbus. The Hispanic community in Columbus was tight-knit, and Carlos knew his host to be an upright man.

"Francisco's name is de Vargas—he traces his ancestors back to the first Spanish to come to Mexico. He is aristocratic, Candy. But we talked about asylum, and if he goes that route, he'd have to leave all that behind him. Conchesca asked Carlos what good is it for him to buy a senator if he couldn't turn to him for help."

"Oh, boy—I'm sure he didn't like that."

"We had company, so it wasn't loud like their usual arguments, but he told her in no uncertain terms that he didn't 'buy' politicians or call in favors. Francisco heard the simmering anger and winked at me! But he didn't say a word. Carlos agreed to call the senator tomorrow to ask for his assistance, but he thought Francisco has a case for asylum."

"That sounds promising."

"I could tell Carlos was eager to end their argument in their usual way—making wild, passionate love—so I took Francisco home. He's staying in a gorgeous place."

When Mérida popped her head into the shop the next morning before it opened, Candy asked her the question that had been simmering in her mind all night long, "What's the next step?"

"Carlos is going to get back with him today, after we get some advice." Mérida paused, looking down. She smiled at her best friend. "He is staying with José Morales; he's a distant cousin and a prominent member of the Hispanic community. That influenced Carlos. I spent the night there after one glass of imported Spanish brandy. Powerful stuff. Apparently, Francisco carried me upstairs—and I missed it!" She sighed.

"He must be something else. Girl, you're dreamy."

"I can't wait for you to meet him. He's like something out of a movie!" She giggled. "Carlos called about midnight, when he saw my car wasn't home. At breakfast, Francisco told me he was relieved to be able to tell him where I was. His cousin's wife got on the phone to assure Carlos she'd put me to bed. I woke up in this fabulous gown, in a heavenly room, and I didn't remember a thing. My clothes, neatly washed and pressed, lay at the foot of the bed."

"I wondered; I've never seen you wear the same outfit two days in a row."

"I have a ton of stuff to do today—two deadlines. I didn't have time to go change. I'm out of here."

Candy thought about Mérida's quandary all morning, and at lunch, she went over to the main office to see what was going on. When she looked into Mérida's suite, she literally gasped. A beautiful man, giving new meaning to the phrase "tall, dark, and handsome," leaned over her friend. He pointed to something on a print-out, and Mérida nodded and told him he was right and flashed him a brilliant smile. Candy cleared her throat, holding back a grin at the one who had so vehemently sworn off men a year ago. "I thought you had two deadlines, and I find you flirting with a handsome stranger."

Mérida turned her chair around. "You pig! Francisco is helping me to meet those deadlines. One has already been sent off." She stood and held her hand out. "Come meet Francisco de Vargas, my new assistant. Francisco, my very best friend, Candy Long, who owns Candy's Cuts and Curls next door."

Francisco met her halfway across the room, drawing her hand up and kissing it as Mérida told him about her gringa sister, her stepmother's daughter-in-law.

"We are a complicated family," Candy said, "but I'm a trailer park girl from Mississippi. I certainly don't deserve to be treated like royalty."

"Mexico swore off royalty when we won our independence, Candy. We are in the Americas."

"I came to find out the latest news, Mérida. Has Carlos heard anything?"

"He has. He and Francisco will be flying to Washington tomorrow. The Border Patrol is excited to find someone who can testify about the murder of one of their own, and the senator thinks we can make a good case for asylum."

A cloud crossed Francisco's handsome face, though he quickly tried to erase it.

"If you do that, you'll leave your home and all you are behind, won't you?" Candy sympathized, touching his arm and looking closely at him, her wide grey eyes swimming with tears.

"I heard hairdressers were social workers in disguise. You see my soul. But, Miss Candy, I will be alive, and the U.S.A. is not such a bad place to live. Ernesto has lived here a long time and only rarely comes back to Mexico. His father was a good politician—one of those rare Mexican government officials, he was not corrupt—and he paid for it with his life. My cousin had business connections here, and he thought it prudent to bring his family to this country. He has been a citizen for many years."

Mérida thrust some advertising fliers in her hands. "Look at these and tell me he's not a genius!"

Candy admired the creativity of the work. "You will meet your deadlines and win your bid with this, Mer."

"I know. Are you at lunch? When is your next appointment?" Mérida caught Candy's arm and turned her to the kitchen. "Let's see what we can scrounge up." She looked back over her shoulder. "Are you hungry, Francisco?"

Francisco Goes to Washington

The next morning, Carlos leased a plane to fly to D.C. to avoid showing IDs and Francisco's passport. The senator had a car waiting, and they were quickly whisked away to his office to meet with several Border Patrol and DEA agents. Homeland Security was there also, and they gave the senator a dossier on Francisco Antonio Morales de la Vargas. The border patrol quickly ascertained that Francisco did have the information they needed to apprehend the men who had shot their agent. DEA men assured him that with his help, they could bring down a significant cartel.

"But what about his life? They're already after him," Carlos questioned. "They haven't traced him to Columbus so far, but..."

"We can give him asylum, and we're good at witness protection, Mr. Rodriguez. Now we must create a new identity. We will stage a fake death of Mr. Vargas and put the story in the newspapers in Mexico. What shall your new name be?"

"Give him mine. Papá has so many kids one more will hardly be noticeable."

"Rodriguez," Francisco affirmed. "I will be a modern man and take my wife's name."

Carlos cocked an eyebrow, a smile twitching at the corners of his mouth.

"Have you married, Mr. Vargas?" one of the agents asked.

"Not yet, but a certain Señorita Rodriguez has bewitched me. She is creative, brilliant in her field, which we happen to share, and also beautiful."

"Fine then, Rodriguez it will be, and good luck in your pursuit of this woman whose name you're taking. Now, for a first name—you have plenty to choose from, but they might trace the Morales to your cousin."

They settled on Antonio, coupled with Carlos's mother's maiden name, and the agents promised a new passport and citizenship in forty-eight hours. The senator, Carlos's friend, swore him in, in his office. Creating a résumé might take a bit more time, but it would be done. Francisco spent several hours at the DEA offices helping identify the shooters and describing the incident he had witnessed. They flew home late that afternoon.

"You have given me a day of your life and powerful connections, Carlos. How can I thank you?"

"Love my sister well." Carlos looked steadily at this man, yesterday a stranger, today known to him as a brave and noble man who was giving up his entire past to bring evil to justice.

"This is a command I look forward to obeying," Francisco replied.

"Why don't you rest? It's has been a grueling day for you. I'm sorry about your mamá. Mine, too, died of cancer."

Francisco's eyes blurred, and he swiped a hand across them. "Perhaps I could close my eyes a minute."

He heard Carlos's chuckle and his warning about a certain bundle of energy who would be wanting to celebrate the news they hadn't been allowed to share by phone or text beyond, "It's all good."

When they got into Columbus, a quick call informed them Mérida was at Candy's house, so Carlos dropped him off and went on home.

Francisco immediately warmed to Joe Long and the two little boys. He learned the younger, Rodney, was called "Rod," after Mérida's father and Joe's father-in-law, who had somehow saved Candy's life. The description of the events in Washington waited until after dinner, when the boys were in bed. While Candy and Joe were upstairs with their sons, Francisco asked Mérida if she could get used to calling him Antonio.

"And what will your last name be?"

His eyes twinkled as he informed her he would be taking his wife's name. Her eyes flared, but before he allowed the steam to mount, he said, "Rodriguez."

"Isn't that the most politically correct decision?" he added.

"My name? But... Are you saying..."

Francisco took her in his arms, and the kiss they shared caused all her doubts to flee.

"This is too soon," Mérida murmured.

"This is not soon enough. I have waited all my life for you. I have seen you in my dreams. We will wait a respectable time—perhaps next week?" Francisco ran his long, elegant fingers down the side of her soft cheek, reaching under her chin to tip her face up for another kiss. "I only regret we cannot plan an elegant wedding. I must keep everything low-key to avoid unwanted attention."

"We only need to be married. Who needs a fancy wedding when I have a perfect groom? I will call you Antonio because I want you safe, but in our bed, you will always be Francisco."

"We got the kids down, now we want the full story," Joe said as he and Candy waited for the couple to disentangle themselves. "Why does this family always know from the minute they lay eyes on someone that they are joined for life?"

Candy poked him. "You did not, Joe Long! The first time you saw me, I was horrible."

"Ah, but when I closed my eyes, I saw those haunted grey eyes. And when you came to class, and I saw you had been born again, I was a goner."

"I still looked awful—bleached hair, terrible clothes..." Candy's protests were cut off by a gentle kiss.

"Hush, Woman," Joe whispered, looking down at his wife.

Francisco felt love in this room, in this family. The night before last, he felt passion sizzle between Carlos and Conchesca. God was drawing him into a loving family, giving him back all he feared he would lose.

"I hear a story there," Francisco said.

"But not one for tonight. We must hear everything about you," Candy insisted.

Francisco thought this was a strange pair of best friends, this fair gringa and his flashing black-eyed, brown-skinned lady love. But he knew the devotion between them was genuine, and they shared confidences, so he outlined the plan. Once again, he saw sympathy flash in Candy's eyes as she pondered all he would lose.

"They're going to stage a death? You'll never see your family again?"

"It will work. I can draw up a new will and leave everything to my cousin, Enrico. After the Mexican government takes more than their share, it will be transferred here. My sisters and brothers can visit their cousin here, but you're right, I can never go home."

"Mérida knows I didn't have anything to go home to, but the Rodriguez family brings everyone into their circle of love," Candy said. "You'll have a wonderful family here."

"Rod is the father I never had—he married my mother and taught us all to love and trust," Joe added. "It's a good family, and I gather you want to join us."

"Daddy?"

Joe excused himself and crossed to the foot of the stairs. "Why are you still up, Eddie?"

"I have Abuelo's knife. I didn't mean to steal it, Daddy, honest. It ended up in my pocket after we carved some birds."

Joe climbed the stairs and took his son back to bed. "We'll give it to him tomorrow. Now it is sleep time, Young Man." Their soft words disappeared into the bedroom.

"Abuelo is the head of this family. I must make my case before him."

"He wants all his children to be happily married. Promise him babies, and he will welcome you!" Candy laughed. "Lots and lots of babies, huh, Mer?"

Mérida blushed. "You are such a pig, Candy. I can't believe you said that!"

Candy smiled. "I'm happy for you, and I'm sure you will have no problem giving this handsome man lots of beautiful babies."

"Would you quit?" Mérida couldn't look at Francisco, but he winked at Candy.

"Sounds like a good plan—but first I must ask the papá, right?"

Mérida paused and took a deep breath. "As soon as you're legal. Papá hates illegals."

"Shouldn't be long. They promised a packet in forty-eight hours. Soon I will be someone else."

"I'm not the same person I once was, before I met this family," Candy said. "What are we to call you—Antonio?"

Francisco nodded. "Antonio," he repeated, as if he were trying it on for size.

Joe walked across the room and held out his hand. "Antonio Rodriguez, welcome to the family."

Mérida's phone dinged, and she looked down at a text from Carlos. "Tomorrow night, Papá and Martha are coming to Carlos's house for dinner; they want us to come. Shall I say yes?"

"I can't ask him for your hand this soon."

"Circumstances are a bit usual, I think," Joe said, "and besides, he married my mother, what? Less than two months after they met? I got back after a one week honeymoon and he told me he loved her. Yep, that's the way this family works."

Francisco turned to Mérida. "I must wait two months for you?"

"Dinner—it's dinner I'm asking about."

Chuckling, Francisco tangled his fingers in her hair. "Sí, we'll go to dinner, if you promise to protect me. You are his baby."

"She was his poor, motherless child—ten years old when her mother died," Joe said.

Francisco groaned. "Make this harder, why don't you?"

They laughed, but Candy leaned over to pat his hand. "Rod is a firm believer in marriage, and he still acts like a newlywed himself. It'll be fine."

Francisco was tired, but as he left, he complimented the Longs on their children. "Eddie looks like his mother, Joe, but he certainly has your mannerisms. I can see you are a fine father. Miss Candy," once again he brought her fingers to his lips. "A mother after God's own heart."

Mérida dropped him off, refusing his offer to come in because she knew he was tired. When she pulled into her driveway, Carlos stepped out of his backdoor.

He called across the yard, and she floated across the yard, smiling.

"Did he tell you his new name, and why he chose it?"

Conchesca appeared at her husband's shoulder. "Come tell us everything. This is the most romantic thing I've ever heard. Spanish nobility swept off his feet by my little sister-in-law."

"It is too soon, isn't it, Hermano?"

Carlos put his arm around Mérida and brought her into the house. "Café, little sister? Maybe some Spanish brandy?" She elbowed him, and he laughed. "In D.C. I saw a most thorough dossier on Francisco Antonio Morales de Vargas, and I assure you I know the details of his life: when he was potty trained, the schools he attended, his family, his jobs and hobbies, his many mistresses..."

"Carlos!" his wife reprimanded. "That is not so, Mérida! He told me not one hint of scandal. How could you say that?" She frowned at him.

Carlos chuckled as the anxiety he'd created turned into fury and his sister turned on him. He held his hands up, laughing. "Conchesca is right; he is an upright and moral man, from an outstanding family. I wish we could show it to Papá, but from now on he is Antonio Lorenzo Degas Rodriguez."

"He chose Mamá's maiden name?"

"I kind of supplied that one, but he chose his wife's last name—said he was a modern American man, grabbing his wife's name and reputation for excellence in his field."

"He did?" Mérida beamed.

Carlos put his arm around his sister. "He did. He told the agents he wasn't married yet, but a certain Rodriguez señorita, who was brilliant and beautiful, had stolen his heart." Mérida sighed. "But no one will make you marry this man. I swear I will protect my baby sister."

Mérida started to protest, but she saw the teasing laughter in his eyes. "You approve, my brother?"

"He is a fine, brave man. He stayed with his mother through her treatment and death, despite the danger to himself. Honestly, I have all the respect in the world for him."

"Tell me about this paragon of virtue, Mer," Conchesca said.

"He's tall and very slender, with an air of nobility about him. His résumé is impressive, and his work is genius. He will be an asset to the office."

"Oh, so that's why you are attracted to him—he brings talent to your firm?" Conchesca winked at her husband.

Carlos laughed then. "I don't think so. All we have to tell Papá is that he's already carried her off to bed, and he will either kill him or march him to the altar."

"Carlos Rodriguez, you know it wasn't like that!"

"Did he, or did he not, carry you to bed?"

"I don't remember, but I woke up in the most beautiful bedroom. The curtains were of the finest white lace."

"And you were wearing?"

"A gown of softest silk." She stopped, seeing her brother raise his eyebrows with a grin and a shrug. "His cousin's wife put me to bed!" she protested.

"And you are sure of this?"

Mérida flew at him. "You are a beast of a big brother!"

Carlos laughed. "I'm sorry, Little One. I'm teasing you, and if Francis—Antonio—were here, he'd challenge me to a duel to defend your honor. The man has an impenetrable moral code. Papá will like him, Mer."

"Even if he is illegal?" she whispered.

"The circumstances are such that Papá will honor him. He is a brave, fine man, Mérida."

She sighed. "I want tomorrow night behind me."

"Stop by Martha's tomorrow. Talk to her and tell her. She knows how to handle Papá."

Mario's Baby

Rod and Martha arrived at Carlos's house at five. He turned around, looking. "Where is he?"

"Good evening, Papá," Carlos greeted him. "Come in. Mérida and Antonio will be here at six. I wanted to talk to you first, and give you the background on the man you will know as Antonio Lorenzo Degas Rodriguez."

"You gave him our name? Your mother's name and my name?"

"He will be the first Rodriguez to spring from nobility. His family came from Spain to the New World when the first noble families got land grants. He is a fine, good man, Papá."

"He is illegal."

"With good cause. Sit, and I will tell you." Carlos told his father about the trip to Washington, the interviews with the DEA and Border Patrol, and the courage of this man as he bravely stood beside his dying mother while assassins sought to track him. "He saw the murder of one of our agents. He is going to testify and break up a huge cartel, Papá, and our government will give him a new identity and asylum here in exchange."

"You like this man?"

"I do. I read a detailed dossier on him. I told Mérida he's been thoroughly vetted, and he is squeaky clean. I watched him endure cross-examinations until a lesser man would have cracked." He handed his father a purged résumé and some samples of his work.

"Mérida has been looking for some help, and he applied for the job. He's quite well-trained, and very talented, wouldn't you say?"

Martha looked over Rod's shoulder. "Oh, my, this is lovely, isn't it?"

"Why the name, Carlos?"

Carlos grinned. "I suggested it, and he agreed. He said he would be a modern American and take the name of his wife."

Rod looked closely at Carlos.

"They asked him if he had married, and he said no, but he had met a beautiful Rodriguez señorita who was brilliant and talented. They wished him luck in his pursuit, and urged him to marry quickly."

"And Mérida—she is sure of this, and she only met him four days ago?"

"Mario," Martha began, but Carlos interrupted.

"How long did it take you to know you loved Martha, Papá?"

"Those were life and death circumstances. I could tell she was a woman of character."

"And these are not the same, Husband?" Martha rested her hand on his arm. He covered it with his own and looked at her with adoration.

"You didn't have a dossier on me, love, and I certainly didn't come from nobility! I was the daughter of moonshiners, and the wife of…"

He put a finger on her lips. "Shh, that's enough. We will meet this man."

"And if your daughter loves him?"

"If he loves her well, we will welcome him. But, remember, she is my baby."

"I told him the same thing when he asked how he could thank me. I told him to love my sister well. He replied he looked forward to being obedient to that command. I believe he is a gift from God for our Mérida."

The doorbell rang, but before Carlos could answer, Mérida pushed it open. "Papá, I'd like you to meet Antonio."

A tall man, too masculine to be called beautiful, stepped into the room and crossed quickly to bow before Rod. "Señor Rodriguez," he said.

Rod quickly measured the man, drawing from all Carlos had told him, and said, "Carlos tells me you are the first Rodriguez to be born of nobility. Welcome to the family, Son."

Mérida closed her eyes and let loose a long breath. She shared a look with Martha, mouthing, "Thank you."

Martha merely responded with her quiet smile and took her husband by the hand.

Carlos slipped his arm around his sister. "Abuela was right. God blessed the day He brought Martha to this family," he whispered.

"My daughter swore off men about a year ago," Rod said, "but I see you have managed to change her mind."

"I never believed in love at first sight, Sir. I was wrong. With your permission, I would like to spend the rest of my life loving her well."

"See that you do, Antonio. Now, Carlos, I believe you said you were feeding us?" Rod took Francisco by the arm as they moved to the dining room. "I understand you know Enrico Morales? He is a great friend of the policía. He held a benefit to raise enough money to provide bullet-proof vests for my men. A good man."

"He has been known to my family all my life. He is a distant cousin. I am staying with him."

"How do you feel about being a Protestant, Antonio?" Rod asked.

"Thy people shall be my people. Thy God shall be my God—but then, He is the same God, correct?"

"I've made an appointment for them to talk to pastor tomorrow. We should have his packet by Thursday," Carlos said.

When the young couple left, Rod took Martha's hand and started to follow them, but Carlos caught his arm.

"Can you stay a minute, Papá?" Rod's son looked anxious, so he agreed. "Conchesca was making photos of the wedding, and I have something I want you to see."

He walked over to the bookcase and reached down a packet. "We all were taking cell phone pictures, and some are not too clear, but a couple of them concern me." He thumbed through the pictures he had printed out and handed his father several.

Rod studied them and drew out of his pocket a magnifying glass he used to examine evidence. "It is him, I think."

"Who?" Conchesca crowded over his shoulder and looked. She turned pale and whispered, "Jeffery. Jeffery was spying on the wedding."

"I need these. We will blow up the plates and find him. This is not good, Carlos."

"I haven't told her yet."

"You must, and John, too. We must watch over her."

"That's what this family does, Papá. We'll circle the wagons."

A Simple Affair

The packet did arrive as promised, and Antonio and Mérida quickly applied for a marriage license. By Sunday afternoon, in a quiet ceremony in Rod and Martha's house, the family heard the name Francisco Antonio Morales de Vargas for the first and last time, as he became Antonio Lorenzo Degas Rodriguez.

After the wedding, Carlos and Rod took John into Rod's study to give him the details of Jacinta's ill-fated relationship and the photos of his car. Rod had the lab examine the photos and obtain the license plate. Rod warned him this was a dangerous man, a mentally unbalanced man, and they thought through ways to protect her. They agreed it would be better to live in her apartment in the gated community, for the time being. When she argued about leaving his home, he reluctantly told her about the photos, but they only told the girls they wanted to use the pool at her place.

Antonio and his bride lived in the carriage house until his money arrived from Mexico, and he built Mérida a beautiful Spanish style home in a new section of Columbus, just beyond Conlos Corners. They worked well together, except when Mérida fussed, but then they kissed and made up—sometimes she pretended to disagree, just so they could make up.

Hope House Reunion

One night, long after the boys were asleep, Candy lay in Joe's arms and asked him if he was still awake. He replied, "Barely, why?."

"I've been thinking."

Pulling her a bit closer, he kissed her temple. "That's always dangerous."

"Unless I'm thinking about you, right?"

"Unless you are thinking positively about me."

"I always think positively about you. You're a wonderful husband, and a terrific father."

"Thank you, Baby. I'm glad you never get mad at me."

"That might be stretching it. Do you want to know what I'm thinking about or not?"

"Does this require a lights-on moment?"

"Not really. I want to organize a Hope House Reunion. I haven't seen Missy since Eddie was in preschool."

"She's the farthest away; Laura and her husband are the only ones in town, finishing up his last year of seminary. Cathy and her husband are still in school in Illinois, right?"

"And Michelle is in her residency at Cleveland Clinic."

"What's Missy up to these days?"

"She just took a job with Lowes in Elkins. When she graduated from WVU—in three years—she started at Penney's in a town about forty miles south of the university, and then moved to a Lowe's closer to home. She's really happy to be home. She's bought a small house—calls it her doll house."

"Too bad all the Rodriguez boys have gotten married. They are good men, and we'd have her in the family."

"She'd never leave her mountains. We owe her. I'm a Christian because of her, and I couldn't have gotten my GED without her help."

"But you aced beauty school on your own."

"Because your mom helped with Eddie, and you studied beside me every night."

"We worked hard those early years. What are you thinking? When, where?"

"I'll call Beth next week and send out an email to everybody."

"I hope we can pull it off. It'd be fun." Joe punched his pillow. "Now can we go to sleep?"

"I love you, Joe."

Joe pulled her into a spoon. "I'm glad. You're the best thing that ever happened to me."

Candy put her hands over his, and they drifted off to sleep.

The next week, emails started flying back and forth. The consensus they reached was Labor Day Weekend, and Candy began searching for a venue. After dropping off Eddie at school and young Rod at home with Martha, she sat with Carlos and Conchesca having a cup of coffee at their office. Carlos was thinking about adding another row of spaces across the back of Conlos Corners. Joe and Juan both needed to expand, and they could easily use up much of the new building. John Gilbert, Jacinta's husband, was thinking of adding kitchen and bath remodeling, and Candy dreamed of a day spa, offering body wraps and facials. She had squeezed a pedicure chair into the shop, but it was crowded.

"I've been in touch with my Hope House friends. Cathy and her husband want to open a counseling office here in Columbus. Cathy has her masters in social work, and her husband finishes his PhD in psychology in December. They want to set up an office together."

"We could build to suit—tell them to contact us. Now that Antonio has joined Mérida, their graphic design and printing shop is humming," Carlos said. "They need to add space."

Conchesca, the keeper of the books, said, "That just about fills us up with the back row. I'm going to have to hire, too, to keep up with all these new folks in the expansion. If you could have what you want, Candy, with your day spa, how much space would you require? The jeweler on the end told us he wants to retire, so we can enlarge beside and behind."

"I'd have to hire an esthetician and a masseuse, so I'll need rooms for each of them. I need manicure stations and pedicure chairs. But, guys, I'd be walking on water. I'm in the black in the shop, but to take on all this is a big risk." Candy ran her fingers through her soft brown hair. "Joe and I will have to pray about this."

"Maybe he could find another boatload of rejects he can easily fix." Carlos chuckled. "He financed his whole launch with that little deal."

"Joe and I were talking last night. It's amazing how something as horrible as killing his father was such a blessing for us. I never knew the love of a family—without the Rodriguez family, Joe wouldn't have a job, much less his store, and I wouldn't have my own shop. We owe you guys, big time."

"Martha has gotten Papá out of our daily business! She eased the way for Antonio, and Carlos reminded Mérida of what Abuela told us at Christmas. We are the ones who are grateful," Conchesca said, standing to hug Candy.

"Oh, and we need to add Mom's business to that list of blessings you guys have given us."

"She's making money hand over fist. She needs to hire a seamstress, but finding someone up to her standards is impossible. Can you talk to her? Couldn't she hire someone to do the grunt work and retain the finishing touches?"

"She's mentioned what fine work Alexandra does," Candy said.

"Alexandra loves to work with her. She is not a scholar, our Alexandra. She is too kinetic, too hands on, but Martha teaches her patiently and says she is good. Perhaps she will be a seamstress and work with her grandmother. She's been a good grandmother for all our children. They bask in her praise, and she's generous with it. But she doesn't let them get away with a thing!"

"When all she and Joe had was a poor apartment, she didn't hesitate to take me in and love me like a daughter. She and Rod do a fine thing with the Boys' Club, and she wants a girls' program."

"Papá will have to retire to keep up with her." Carlos stood to go to his office, but before he left he asked if her plumbing problem was settled.

"So far, so good. I gotta run. I'm late. Love you guys." Candy went out their main door, then went next door to Candy's Cuts and Curls. Nancy had opened up, and Misty would be in soon. As she always did when she walked into her business, she whispered a prayer of thanksgiving.

Glancing at her book, Candy noted Beth, the counselor from Hope House, would be in around ten. *Good, I can talk to her about the reunion.* Candy looked up from the haircut she was giving when Beth walked in.

"I'll be ready in a few," she said.

"I'm a few minutes early," Beth said. They exchanged pleasantries while Candy whirled the chair around and handed her client a hand mirror to check the back of her head. When she announced it was perfect, Candy unsnapped the grey cape and led her to the desk to check her out. Beth arranged herself on the chair and waited.

"You ready for me to do those highlights, Beth?"

Beth checked her watch. She was interviewing a new girl today, so she suggested next time.

Candy asked Beth about her plan to have a reunion over Labor Day weekend, adding, "Everyone's a go except Michelle. She's not sure she can get off."

"I haven't seen Missy since Eddie was a baby," Beth said. "Cathy and David come in whenever they're in town. Have you met Cathy's husband?"

"Yes. Can you believe she married a psychologist? Our cheerleader ended up with a degree in women's ministry, married to a preacher; Cathy has a degree in counseling, and is married to a psychologist! God makes all things new."

"God did quite a bit of work that summer. John and I have said that summer was a time of miracles—so many deeply wounded girls."

"Cathy and her husband plan to set up a joint practice here in Columbus. My brother-in-law is building to suit them. Everyone is happily settled—

except Missy. She hasn't met anyone to share her life with yet, and I worry about her. She told me maybe she'd never get married. I don't think she's dealt with the rape. I've told her loving the right man is a beautiful thing. If Mom can find happiness with Rod, after brutal abuse for fifteen years, anyone can be healed."

"That family has meant a lot to all of you," Beth said.

"You got that right! We've been taken in by this great, big, wonderful family. Joe and I can never repay them."

"You don't realize what a blessing you are, Candy. I'll tell my family we have to be here for Labor Day weekend. I can't miss the reunion!"

Labor Day weekend rolled around. Cathy and her husband stayed with Carlos and Conchesca, and a very pregnant Laura and her husband were at Mérida's, even though they lived on the other side of Columbus. Carlos was able to draw up some plans for the counseling office at Conlos Corners while Cathy and her husband were in for the weekend.

Michelle was able to get one day off, but had to leave early Monday morning to return to Cleveland Clinic. She stayed at Beth's, and Missy was with Candy and Joe. Candy got free decorating advice, and the girls even spent some time in used furniture stores and yard sales. Candy couldn't believe how Missy spotted stuff that looked like junk to her. She purchased a brass lamp black with age and used ketchup to remove the layers of neglect. It turned out to be a bright brass, with graceful curves absolutely perfect for the front hall. She insisted a love seat had "elegant lines," and hauled it to an upholstery shop in Joe's truck. When Candy picked it up two weeks later, she was astounded by its transformation.

Missy got in late Friday night, and Candy stayed in the guest room with her so they could whisper all night. Candy got out her photo albums, and they pored over them. Joe corralled the boys Saturday morning, fixing pancakes so Mommy could sleep late. He took Eddie into the shop with him, and dropped little Rod off with his mom.

Michelle arrived Saturday evening. Carlos insisted on reserving a nice room in a downtown hotel, and paying for their meal Saturday night. The Rodriguez family crashed the party, so their clan out-numbered the Hope House girls and their husbands. Each of the women told her story, paying tribute to their time at Hope House, the wise and gentle counsel of Beth and John, and the unconditional support of their housemother, Miss Ginny. They completed their testimonies by sharing their lives post-Hope House. God had intervened in each life, providing scholarships, opportunities, and love to them all.

Joe had become a part of Hope House; he and Candy fell in love while she lived there, and they had been married at the maternity home. Michelle made everyone laugh describing Joe staring at Candy during GED classes, and the girls teased Candy about blushing every time they mentioned his name. Martha shared the memories of her son and his very pregnant bride, and agreed with them when they credited their success to the generosity and love of Rod's family. Once again, the Rodriguez family members were overwhelmed with gratitude for the sacrifices made by their parents and grandparents that had afforded them a comfortable life and unwavering love.

With final hugs and laughter, the reunion broke up Monday morning, all of them promising one another to do it again, and often. As the out-of-towners pulled off, Candy wept and Joe drew her into his arms, holding her tightly.

"We need to do something to pay it forward for Hope House," Joe said.

"You mean in addition to rewiring that old building?" Candy asked.

"What a job! And how about your free hair styles for all the girls, Candy?"

"That's such a little thing. I remember what it meant to me when Michelle's father paid for me to go to the beauty shop. I'd never been in a salon before."

"Hoo-boy, I remember when you walked into class that Monday. You were a vision."

"Michelle said your tongue hung out," Candy teased.

"I don't doubt it—and you get more beautiful every year."

"Flattery will get you everywhere."

"You mean I'll get lucky tonight?"

"You are lucky every night."

"I know," he said as he lowered his lips to hers.

School Violence

Juan got a call from Carlos, who had received a call from the police station. Rod was briefing his men on the upcoming day when the 911 call came in—a shooter at an elementary school. He realized with horror that it was Jacinta's school. Nearby cars had raced to the scene, and those on scene were reporting teachers were putting their students under desks and locking classroom doors. It was apparently a lone shooter, but he was in a third-grade classroom; Jacinta taught third grade.

One of the officers reported Rod took off on a run, taking a police car and driving full out, sirens blaring and lights flashing. He screeched to a halt, bending low and scrambling to the line of county cars to talk with his men. They had a hasty conference and called in a sniper. Then Rod moved off, bent double. He knew the building, and he prayed the janitor's door was open in the back. It was. Easing himself into the building, he pulled his gun, shoved a loaded clip into it, and held it up in the air as he dodged around corners.

The Rodriguez family grapevine buzzed furiously. Joe was out on a job, but Juan closed his store and drove to his father's home. He didn't want Martha to be by herself if she heard anything on the news. The sewing business now took up two rooms, and a young Hispanic woman looked up from her machine as he ran up the stairs. Realizing the ladies were not listening to the radio nor watching the news on TV, he slowed and took a deep breath.

"Juan, what is it, Dear?" Martha crossed the room. "Is something wrong?"

He put his arm around her shoulder. "Something is going down at Jacinta's school. Papá has gone over there."

Martha's hand fluttered to her chest, but she remained calm.

No wonder his papá loved this stoic woman. Knowing her history as he did, Juan knew her to be a woman of courage. Maybe he needed her more than she needed him.

"We should turn on the TV," she said, and led him downstairs. She turned on the set in the family room and backed up to the couch. Juan lowered himself beside her and took her hand. "Where is he? I don't see him with the other officers."

"I don't know." Frantic texts were beeping on cell phones. Carlos and his brothers tried to remain at work, knowing they'd be in the way at the scene. But soon, unable to accomplish anything, they all gathered at Carlos's office. Candy stood in front of the TV, gnawing on her knuckles and wishing Joe were here—no, she wanted him to be with his mother. Conchesca sat on the sofa, staring and praying. Carlos led them in a prayer. Mérida reached for Candy's hand. Antonio came up behind her, placing his hands on her shoulders. She leaned against him, blinking back tears. His arms circled her.

Candy noticed his hand covered her belly and suddenly realized her friend was fearing her sister and father would never see the child she carried. "They're going to be okay, Mer. I know they are," Candy whispered.

"Where is he, Carlos?" Mérida's husband asked.

"I don't know. I can't see anything but a bunch of guys in blue. That guy over there is the police sniper, but I don't see Papá. Juan went to be with Martha, and I sent a text to Joe." His phone beeped. "Joe's on his way to the house."

"Where's John?" Mérida asked.

"He's there, poor guy," Carlos said, and led them in another prayer for their brother-in-law.

At the school, Rod had made his way inside through the janitor's back door. He inched down the hallway, ducking under each window. He knew where his daughter's classroom was, and he moved slowly and stealthily in that direction. He cut off his walkie-talkie, not wanting any noise as he approached her door. He inched up, peering into the window. Thank God;

Jacinta saw him. She talked quietly, soothing the children, and walked to the back of the classroom to turn the children's eyes away from the door. The shooter told her to shut up and come here. Rod winced. The guy's voice was shrill with hysteria. He took a deep breath and said a quick prayer.

Jacinta instructed the children to stay as they were and walked back to stand beside the shooter, asking him what he wanted to distract him. The moment her father's body crashed against the door, she raised up her heel and brought it down hard on the man's foot. He doubled over, but raised his gun toward her. He dropped before getting off a shot. Rod moved quickly toward the body and checked for a pulse while Jacinta gathered the crying children in her arms.

"It's all over, Kids," Rod said. "Your mommies are outside." He flipped on his walkie-talkie. "Shooter down. Stand down, threat eliminated. I repeat, stand down. We have some kiddies who need their mommies, and we're bringing them out."

Jacinta made the children stand in their usual rows, knowing their ordinary routine would be calming. She marched them down the hall as police officers went to the office and into every classroom, bringing calm. She kept her class quiet, putting her finger to her lips, and saw each of her students into the waiting arms of a parent before falling into John's arms. His daughters were soon in the circle of their love. Once they were aware that this was the teacher and it was her classroom the shooter had been in, the TV cameras focused on them. She realized if she kept talking, the children in her class could be moved away unobtrusively, so she answered their questions.

"How did you stay calm, Mrs. Gilbert?" one reporter called.

"I knew my papá would come for me," she said. "Officer Rodriguez is my father."

Of course school was closed for the day; once all the children were safely away, she returned for her pocketbook. A yellow tape across her door sealed off the crime scene. The body was already tagged and in a body bag. An investigating officer handed her the pocketbook she sought. "I can identify the shooter," she said.

"You know him?"

"I dated him about a year ago. His name is Jeffery Maloney. Papá can give you his rap sheet."

"Are you okay?"

"Yes, my husband is pulling the car up."

John brought the truck closer; he'd left it a block away when he ran to the school. Putting his girls in the car, he turned the vehicle around to take his family home.

Jacinta pawed through her purse to catch the incoming text. *Where are you, Sis?*

She replied they were on the way home. She glanced up to her husband. "They are all gathering at Papá's. Shall we go there?"

"Yes!" screamed the girls from the back seat.

After agreeing with his children, John said, "Poor Martha."

"Juan went over there the minute he heard," Jacinta reported.

"You have an amazing family, Baby."

"I do. I listened to those Hope House girls last weekend, and I realized how special they are. When Joe and Candy gave us credit for their success, I thought they would have made it anywhere. I've never met such hard-working, brave people as those three." She reminded John about Martha's freedom quilt. "I had given up on Mérida. I thought she was going to be a spoiled brat all of her life, but Candy changed her."

"I can't imagine your father without Martha. He leans on her—and he's a strong guy."

"She is a wise and gentle woman. All of us seek her advice. She told me to marry you."

"A wise woman indeed. I'll have to thank her for that." He glanced over at his wife and reached for her hand. "It's over, Jacinta. No more dead calls."

"In the classroom, he said if he couldn't have me, no one would."

When they pulled up in front of Rod's house, brothers and sisters spilled out. They pulled Jacinta into their arms and held her. The spicy scent of Mexican food greeted them as they walked inside. Abuela had taught them well. Their parents had been poor, but even if they only had beans and rice, food was there to comfort them.

Juan and Joe had put up tables, and chattering women set out lunch. It was a celebration: a fiesta, and the family gathered to rejoice in their safe deliverance. All the businesses were closed or in the hands of underlings this day. Children ran around, oblivious to the crisis and simply soaking up the love.

Martha, in her quiet way, observed, with a heart full of love and thanksgiving. When Candy joined her, she asked, "Did you ever imagine we'd have a family like this?"

"Mom, I never knew families like this existed. I thought you and Joe were pretty wonderful—and you are!" She looked around. "It's still a bit overwhelming, isn't it?"

Martha chuckled. Candy realized her mother-in-law laughed a lot these days. "Yes, but isn't it delightful?"

Overhearing them, Antonio caught Joe's eye. "They are an amazing family, and I'm proud to be in it."

"Me, too, 'Tonio," Joe said, throwing his arm around his elegant friend's shoulder.

Antonio realized he and the gringo electrician were as good friends as his wife and the gringa hairdresser. He felt at home with all these blue-collar workers, and realized what a snob he had been growing up. It was good to be a North American.

"Mamá," Ricardo shouted over the din, "what do you hear from Papá?"

"He is fine, not a scratch, he says, but busy."

"How did it go down, 'Cinta?" Tomás wanted to know.

Jacinta told him how she happened to see her father peek in the window, and had tried to create a distraction. When her father crashed through the door, she stepped hard on the shooter's foot with her high heels.

"I knew those shoes were a lethal weapon," John quipped, and everybody laughed.

"Come, eat," the women urged, waving everyone to the table. Platters of burritos and enchiladas were passed around. All the Rodriguez women kept these ready in their freezers.

Happy chaos reigned. When Rod finally did slip in, no one noticed except John, who walked over to him, put his arms around him, and simply said, "Thank you, Papá."

"Just doing my job, Boy, just doing my job."

Little Rod wasn't sure what had happened, but he knew it was a good thing Abulelo was home, and he wrapped his arms tightly around his grandfather's leg. Rod picked him up, and when everyone realized he was there, they rushed him.

Martha stood quietly back, but his eyes sought her tear-filled ones, and he winked. He knew that all the effusive hugs, enthusiastic slaps on the back, and loud cries were no match for the depth of this woman's love. His chest swelled with gratitude for the wife God had given him.

Before everyone went their separate ways, Rod led his family in prayers of thanksgiving. "God told Jacinta to look at that moment, and He gave her direction. His Spirit kept her peaceful and led me through the halls. May He watch over every home tonight, and grant calm."

Each family left, and each couple found comfort in each other's arms, but none more so than Jacinta and John and Rod and Martha.

Despite the sweetness of their loving, Rod found his wife in tears. "Qué es, mi amor?"

"I thought you would be safe in a desk job, Mario."

"This was my baby, no?"

"Yes, and you couldn't have done anything different. I tried to trust God, but I was afraid, Mario. To lose you now..."

Rod kissed her eyes, caught each tear with his thumbs, and pulled her close. "I cannot leave you, Cara Mia."

Martha pulled him down for a kiss, and he rejoiced in her confidence, remembering her shyness and her fears the first night of their marriage. He also remembered the second night, when he suggested they make love and her eyes glazed over. She had walked to the bed and lay down, arms stiffly at her side. He was appalled, and sat beside her, talking softly until the terror left her eyes. He took her downstairs and made her tea, and they sat in the family room most of the night. She told him things that night that he didn't want to hear, but she needed to say. She had feared she hadn't pleased him, and he wept, wondering how the human spirit could survive. She finally crawled into his lap and he soothed her hair back from her face. He told her he would never ask for what she was unwilling to give, and she asked him to take her upstairs and love her.

Not only had she survived, awakening to his gentle touch, but now she was a responsive lover and even initiated sometimes. It was good between them.

"Mario, you'll be happy to hear what Jacinta told me."

"Another baby?"

"Yes, she's eight weeks along."

Rod laughed. "He didn't waste much time, did he?"

"You practically gave him an ultimatum at the wedding! Sometimes you can be a bit overbearing, Mario."

"That's why God gave me you—to soften me up, no?"

Martha snuggled to his side, her arm over his torso. He patted it softly.

"I do love you, Mario," she whispered.

"I am glad, beautiful Marta."

The next morning, Martha clung to him as he left, whispering, "Be safe, Mario."

He kissed her softly. "I will come home to you, mi amor."

Rod left work early that night, thinking he might take Martha out for dinner, but when he arrived at the house, he heard giggling women. They were pouring over bridal books and magazines, asking Martha if she could make this or that. He shrugged off his jacket and hung it in the closet. He wondered how anyone could think with all the excited chatter, but his wife was unperturbed, pointing out styles and suggesting fabrics, jotting down colors and patiently explaining why this would work and that wouldn't.

He made his way through the crowd in his living room and closed the door to his office. After a bit, he heard the quiet. He cracked open the door and watched his front door shut.

Martha came to him. "I didn't expect you so early. I'm sorry."

"I came home to take you to dinner."

"This business was your idea, you remember."

"I do, and I'm happy you are doing what you love, creating beauty and making people happy. This is a big job, no?"

"A big wedding: five bridesmaids, a maid of honor, the bride, and a flower girl. But I have six months."

"Six months! Who could wait six months?"

She laughed then. "Not every man is like you, Mario. Couples today don't wait."

"No wonder we have so much divorce! Nothing is sacred." He tugged her by the hand. "Come, mi amor, you have worked enough. Let me take you out—I know a little cantina, where our love began. I will take you there again, and we will remember."

Eddie Comes of Age

Joe heard the bell on the door tinkle and put on his best greet-the-customer face, but it split into a grin when Eddie came in. Then it sobered, when his son's face registered confusion. He walked over and his pre-teen didn't pull away when he drew him into an embrace. He flipped the closed sign over and reached the shade to pull it down.

"What's up, Son?"

Eddie's chin dropped and he studied his battered shoes—Joe couldn't believe what skateboarding did to that kid's shoes. He had to have a new pair every time his father turned around.

Joe dropped his hand to the boy's shoulder and waited. He shared that quality with his mother.

"I found the photo book in the guest room where Aunt Missy stayed, and I was looking through the pictures they were looking at that weekend: the pictures from Hope House."

"Yes?"

"Dad, I saw the pictures of the wedding. You and Mom. And I wondered... She was really far along; with me?"

"Yeah, with you."

"Why did you wait so long to marry her?"

Joe led him over to the counter, pulled out a second stool and perched on it. "She was very young. We had to wait until she turned eighteen. I married her as soon as it was legal and she agreed."

"Oh. But you loved her, right? I mean, you didn't marry her because of me."

"I did, and I am, and I always will be, crazy about your mom. I never loved anyone else. She opened my heart and took every last piece of it until you two boys crowded in."

"At the dinner, they teased you about staring at her in GED class."

"I did. I had a hard time concentrating on our studies."

"But she went to the class from Hope House, and you met her there."

Knowing the conversation he'd never wanted to have was coming, Joe nodded.

"So, she was pregnant when you met her?"

"She was, but I couldn't tell at first. She wore big blouses, but her belly didn't look like it did in those photos."

"So that means you aren't my father?"

"I chose to be your father. I married her before you were born. We fussed over that a bit. She wanted to wait until she was thin, but I insisted so my name would be on the birth certificate, and I would be your legal father. I was there when you were born. I cut the cord. You are, and have been from the time I knew your mother was pregnant, my son. I love you. We married and she came to live with me and Gram. We lived in a little apartment. That was before Gram married Abuelo."

"I get that, Dad, but who was, like, you know, the other one?"

"Your mother was raped, Eddie, so we don't talk about it. You know what that means? When a man over-powers a woman, in this case a mere girl, and she has no choice? Since he assaulted a minor, he was sent to the penitentiary, and inmates—other prisoners—don't like men who hurt little girls. He was killed when you were an infant."

Eddie fidgeted on his stool, clasping his hands. "Did you ever meet him?"

"If I had, I probably would have killed him with my own hands. I had my experiences with a man hurting a woman. My mama, your gram, was abused by my father. He beat her up and raped her, and we didn't escape until he nearly killed her. She was in the hospital for months. I was fifteen, and in foster care until she got out. I saw in your mother the same haunted look: the pain, the shifting of the eyes. It's strange, how victims blame themselves. I couldn't help my mother when I was a boy, but I wanted to rescue your mom. And I fell in love with her warmth, her eagerness to please, her basic goodness. Of course, the fact that she's gorgeous didn't hurt a bit!"

Eddie finally looked up, straight into his father's eyes. "Why didn't she have an abortion?"

"She never considered that. She did think about adoption, but once you started to move and she could feel you, she wanted to keep you. She let me put my hand on her belly, and I felt you move. I used to talk to you before you were born. She wanted her baby, someone who would love her. No one had ever loved her. Her mother was a drunk. Her father died when she was a baby. She never felt loved, and she told me she couldn't give you up. She's a brave one, your mother."

Eddie's eyes misted over. "I guess she's my hero. I should thank her for giving me life, huh?"

"Eddie, you gave her life meaning and purpose. She loves you. I think you know that."

"Yeah, I do, and you do, too. You love me. I should thank you, too; you married a pregnant girl and raised her baby."

"You came as a package deal, Eddie. You and your mom. You two made a man out of me. Come 'ere." Joe held his arms out and drew Eddie into them. He stroked the boy's sun-blond hair and rocked him back and forth.

"I always remember you being my dad, and Abuelo being my grandpa. But it wasn't like that, was it?"

"I've always been your dad, Eddie. Never a choice. You were part of your mother—you share her beautiful grey eyes. I stayed with your mom in the hospital when you were born, and I held you all night. You knew my voice."

"I did?"

"Yep. Your blurry, unfocused eyes searched for your mother, and when she held you and talked to you, you stared at her, drinking her in. Then I touched your cheek and spoke to you and you sought my voice. We connected. My heart burst with love for both of you. I've been proud to have you as my son. You have your mother's gentle spirit. Even when you were two: you tried to throw a tantrum, but never could quite get it off the ground. You'd stop in the middle of your fit and say, 'I dorry, Daddy,' and throw yourself into my arms and cry."

Joe's arms tightened as his boy wept. *God, make my arms Yours. Hold him close to Your heart, and cause him to feel Your love.*

Eddie moved from weeping to sobbing, clinging to Joe, who didn't know what else to do but hold him. When he quieted, Joe shoved a bunch of tissues in his hand. Raising his tear-streaked face, he whispered, "I love you, Dad," and Joe's heart broke.

"I love you, Son. Always have, always will."

"Kinda like God, huh, Dad?"

"Ready to go see your mom? I'm guessing you left Rod down there."

"I've never felt any difference, Dad. You loved me as much as you loved him."

"You, Eddie, are my firstborn. Firstborns make us fathers. We make all our mistakes with our firstborns." Joe jerked his thumb toward the bathroom. "Wanna clean up a bit?"

Eddie came out of the restroom with his face scrubbed, but his red-rimmed eyes were still obvious. Joe held out his arm, and Eddie fitted himself close to his father's side. They walked down to Candy's Cuts and Curls, and she immediately noted her son's state. She smiled brightly over her client's head and said she'd be in the break room in a minute. By the time she got there, the men she loved were clowning affectionately, in their clumsy man-way. They were playing a game of tennis on the Wii she had bought to entertain the boys.

"Where's Rod?" Joe asked.

"He's over with Mérida and the cousins. Antonio bought him a computer art program and blocks. He's quite taken with him. What happened, Eddie?"

"The conversation we knew would happen, Honey," Joe said. "He saw the Hope House photos and asked about our wedding."

Joe saw the fear, the shame, and the anxiety march across his wife's countenance, but before he could say a word, Eddie put his arms around her waist and hugged her.

"Thanks for giving me life, Mom. I love you and Dad so much."

"And we love you, Sweetie. You mean the world to both of us."

"Yeah, I know. Dad's pretty cool, isn't he?"

Candy caught Joe's eye to see how much he had told, and his quick nod told her: everything. Her dark grey eyes spilled over, and she knelt in front of her son. "Your dad loves you, Eddie. I think maybe he married you instead of me."

Joe put his arms around his wife's shoulder. "It was close, Baby. How much longer do you have? I thought we'd go for pizza."

"I'm out of here! I'll let someone else tally up tonight."

After the kids were down, in Joe's arms, in his bed, Candy breathed a sigh. "We made it, Joe, and Eddie's gonna be all right. God answered my prayers beyond everything I could have asked or even thought. Everything I dreamed, everything I hoped for, has come to pass. More than I hoped."

"We still have teenagers ahead of us," Joe replied, "but for tonight, let's enjoy the moment." He pressed a kiss on her brow. "Once, I hoped you would be able to be a wife. I feared you never could, but you certainly exceeded my fondest wishes."

"You taught me to love, Joe." She drew him down for a kiss.

He ran his hands across her body, and her shivers of delight brought a smile to his lips. When she kissed him again and again and pressed against him, he knew he'd love this beautiful, brave woman as long as he had breath.

About the Author

Charlotte met her husband at Duke University. Married in 1962, they reared six children (four natural, one adopted, and one foster daughter). Their nine grandchildren range in age from adults to a toddler, and four are adopted. A pro-life leader for many years, Charlotte believes God creates every child.

A Phi Beta Kappa graduate of Duke, Charlotte received a Masters of Social Work from the University of North Carolina in 1966. She founded a pregnancy help ministry in 1985, and she's been a Mothers of Preschoolers (MOPS) mentor for twenty years. Her experiences as a wife, social worker, mother, pro-life leader, and MOPS mentor contribute to her inspirational fiction.

She lives with her husband, a practicing orthopedic surgeon, in rural West Virginia. She has published articles and short stories, some of them may be viewed at her website/blog: www.charlottesnead.com. She has three novels published by Oak Tara, and many articles and short stories published in various magazines. (Her short stories are free and her books may be purchased at Amazon or at her blog.) She is on Facebook and Twitter @Charlotte Snead.

www.ingramcontent.com/pod-product-compliance
Lightning Source LLC
LaVergne TN
LVHW011419080426
835512LV00005B/148